Primitive
Social
Organization

STUDIES IN ANTHROPOLOGY

Consulting Editors:
MORTON H. FRIED AND
MARVIN HARRIS
Columbia University

Primitive Social Organization

AN EVOLUTIONARY PERSPECTIVE

Second Edition

ELMAN R. SERVICE

UNIVERSITY OF CALIFORNIA,
SANTA BARBARA

RANDOM HOUSE NEW YORK

ISBN: 0–394–31635–5

Library of Congress Catalog Card Number: 78–153198

Manufactured in the United States of America
by The Colonial Press Inc., Clinton, Mass.

Design by Karin Batten

Second Edition

9 8 7 6 5 4

To Professors
Julian H. Steward and Leslie A. White

Editors' Introduction

 Primitive Social Organization is the second in the Random House series of Studies in Anthropology. The original plan was for numbered volumes, whose order of publication would represent the usual order of presentation in most introductions to anthropology. Fortunately, however, the wise counsel of Mr. Charles Lieber prevailed and the paradox of publishing later numbers before earlier ones was avoided. Nevertheless, this volume is one in a series which will ultimately have structural cohesion and even a degree of unity.

There has long been a need for teaching materials suitable for a more advanced introduction to anthropology. Many first-year graduate students of anthropology have already had introductory courses and, in addition, there is an increasing body of laymen who are interested in and knowledgeable about the field. Our plan for the series is a logical outgrowth of this situation. There will be a number of volumes, of variable length, each dealing with a major aspect of anthropology. Each author will acquaint the intelligent beginner thoroughly with his subject but will do so without neglecting his own opinions no matter how controversial they may be. These, then, are not to be cut and dried summaries but, to the extent each subject allows, original views stating the problems and offering highly contemporary "solutions."

This volume by Elman Service meets these requirements admirably, as did the first in the series, *Culture and Personality* by Anthony F. C. Wallace. Professor Service has given both a conventional survey of social organization and stimulating new perspectives. He has cautioned the reader when he is on novel ground, so that even someone new to the field can understand and profit from this book. However, the editors have made no attempt to confine the discussion to basic concepts and orthodox analyses. The more advanced reader will appreciate Service's original insights and hypotheses, knowing that controversy is vital to knowledge and that a clear statement of the alternatives is necessary. Among the many provocative themes which serve this function are Service's preoccupation with specific and general evolutionary perspectives, with the distinction between egocentric and sociocentric systems, with the concept of sodality, with the "natural" categories of relationship, with the differentiation of status from association, and with the exposition of political levels in the context of general evolution.

Anyone who reads more than one book in this series will quickly appreciate the individuality of each author. No attempt has been made to smooth out differences among them. We welcome debate and we trust that, far from discouraging the student, it will encourage him to perfect his knowledge and join in the dialogue.

MORTON H. FRIED AND MARVIN HARRIS

Preface to the Second Edition

The first edition of *Primitive Social Organization* was designed to present, and to test out in an explanatory context, a few concepts and perspectives that derived from, or seemed congenial to, a modern evolutionary theory. It was not intended as a discussion and evaluation of the general academic study of primitive social organization, nor to adjudicate intramural quarrels, nor to "cover the literature." In short, it was intended to be a simple book with only a few messages.

It seems in retrospect, however, that some of the statements that elicited controversy were not intended to do so by the author. This new edition makes occasion to reduce these further to their intended simplicity and to maintain a sharper focus on what the author still sees as the main points. Accordingly, I have modified or deleted some of the more general speculations about the aboriginal ubiquity of the "patrilocal band," the "dominance hierarchy," and the "hierarchical sexuality" of primate groups. It is not relevant to the main argument of the book whether or not those generalities should stand. I have read all the recent works and find now that to be accurate and complete it would be necessary to write and cite at much greater length all the minor exceptions and modifications that different scholars think are required. I chose instead—still in the interest of simplicity—to shorten the argument and avoid the complexities. What the standard aboriginal band was is a factual problem and will never be known for sure. Let us simply agree that it was whatever it was. My feeling that the data and functional logic argued for the likelihood of the patrilocal band was only a surmise—but it was so often regarded by others as my firm conviction that I now willingly give it up. I haven't really changed my mind, but I don't want to be misunderstood any longer.

On the other hand, a conceptual definitional matter—the *sodality*—was denied by some critics because Robert Lowie had once defined it a little differently. I cannot yield to this argument. I needed, and still need, sodality: the only alternative, "a non-residential association with some corporate functions," is far too cumbersome. Sodality is the closest in spirit to this need so it will be retained. Lowie's definition was equally arbitrary, after all, and less useful.

Students, I am told, will be glad of the modifications made in the introductory chapter. There was too much conceptual and definitional argumentation in too little space and the naïve student felt he was being pulled through too tiny a knothole. It was decided to treat some of these evolutionary concepts and perspectives one by one, as they come up in relevant parts of the text, to be brought together again in summary in the final chapter.

Finally, an attempt has been made to discuss or at least cite the most important newer contributions that are related to the major arguments of this book. But again, as claimed for the first edition, to "cover" the academic literature has not been a foremost purpose.

E . R . S .

Preface to the First Edition

In discussing a subject of such enormous scope as primitive social organization one is faced with a choice between two alternative approaches, unless the book is to be itself enormous. One way is to describe the history of scientific thought on the subject, to make a study of the studies. The other way is to disregard most of the controversies that the history of thought always involves and attempt instead to describe primitive social organization more ethnographically, citing from the theoretical literature only the works that relate immediately and directly to the route taken. For better or for worse, the latter approach was chosen here. This decision was made in order to present as straightforwardly as possible a thesis that seems to contribute to the solution of certain fundamental problems. As a text, therefore, the book is one-sided and partial for, as Walter Bagehot said: "To illustrate a principle you must exaggerate much and you must omit much."

Being thus discretionary, the citations alone cannot adequately represent important anthropological contributions to the study of social organization. It is even probable that many works relevant to the particular thesis of this book have been slighted simply because I have not made it a main task to cover the literature. Also, although I have tried to give the actual sources of derivative ideas, some persons are mentioned less often than their importance warrants simply because there is no way to give adequate citation in footnotes for general influence or for personally given aid and comfort. The earliest and most profound of these influences are from my former teachers. I heard about cultural evolution first from Leslie A. White and later, in a different version, from Julian H. Steward. The perspective acquired from them is so basic as to be revealed in the very organization of this book. It is improbable that either White or Steward will agree with all of my interpretations of social organization, however, for some of them diverge from those each of these men has expressed. Although they provided the original evolutionary theories, they should not be blamed for what happened afterward.

The teachings of White and Steward are not alike and many students are partisans of one or the other. I never felt that the two approaches were incompatible; they are distinct largely in that they are relevant to quite different kinds of problems. Marshall Sahlins explained this clearly when he defined General and Specific Evolution to delineate more explicitly their divergent theoretical uses (Sahlins and Service, 1960). This dichotomized evolutionary theory is the basis for nearly all of the more special ideas, notions, and concepts that have been used in the present work. But they did not spring automatically from the broad theory, although at this late point they may seem implicit in it and quite near the surface. Some of the most important of these were precipitated out of discussions (and arguments) with Sahlins, with whom I have been collaborating off and on for some time. He also read the manuscript carefully and made helpful comments, for all of which I am very grateful.

The editors of this series, Morton Fried and Marvin Harris, have given much more time and attention to the manuscript than their editorial duties demanded. Many times during past years I have discussed problems of social organization with Fried and have benefited thereby.

A number of others have given suggestions in later phases of the work. Eric Wolf, Richard N. Adams, and Richard Fox read the manuscript and gave good counsel at many points. Helen S. Service, my wife, has done the same, and also has listened to me talk about it—surely the hardest job of all. Thomas Harding, Arnold Pilling, David Damas, and David Schneider have read parts of the manuscript and made helpful comments.

The more impersonal dependence of this work on certain well-known authorities should be mentioned. In the broadest sense, the works of Émile Durkheim and, of more modern authors, those of Claude Lévi-Strauss, have been important. In neither case, however, does the influence include many of their more special interpretations.[1] There has been a rather similar dependence on the interesting dissertation of Gertrude E. Dole (1957). I have profited from her arduous exploration of the evolution of kinship, but again there is a marked divergence in interpretation at some important points.

These partial discontinuities with the work of eminent scholars, not to speak of the flat disagreement with some others, are enough to make any author nervous. Certainly the reader should be wary for the same reasons. The justification for offering such a work is not that it contains Truth and therefore must prevail, but only that reexaminations and controversies are important in the development of any area of science that makes so much of theory and concepts.

E.R.S.

---

[1] In revising the book, I have not altered this Preface, except for adding the present note. Many people have asked what was, specifically, the debt to Durkheim and Lévi-Strauss, inasmuch as I have criticized both in subsequent publications. Durkheim's anti-individualism (anti-reductionism) in sociological explanation influenced me profoundly when I was a student. Later the derivative anti-genealogical and anti-extensionist perspective on kinship terminology by Lévi-Strauss was helpful at a time in my ignorance when I had thought I was all alone in my disrespect for the prevailing kinship studies in the United States of America.

Contents

Primitive
Social
Organization

1

Introduction

The study of primitive social organization—and particularly of its most intriguing and puzzling aspect, kinship and patterns of kinship nomenclature—has been a central concern in cultural anthropology since its earliest years. L. H. Morgan gave most of his career to his huge study of kinship terminology, *Systems of Consanguinity and Affinity of the Human Family*. Tylor, Durkheim, Maine, McLennan, Bachhofen and others of the nineteenth century also made the study of primitive social organization an important part of their work. There were many weaknesses in their theories, however, in part because of the newness of the study and the paucity of data, but also because of the one-sided character of the prevailing perspective.

In the nineteenth century the usual way of looking at cultural data in the evolutionary context was in terms of stages or levels alone. With the exception of some of Durkheim's work, there was little concern with cultures in the particular or specific sense—that is, *the* culture of a given society—or with social systems as such. Consequently certain characteristics of social organizations were not understood.

In our century numerous advances have been made, most

strikingly since theories of functionalism became influential. Several French, Dutch, and American anthropologists influenced by this current have made contributions by considering more fully the systemic nature of particular societies. British social anthropologists, however, have most consistently and fully carried out structural-functional analysis. So completely have they concentrated on particular societies, and hence so far are they from the nineteenth-century evolutionary perspective, that they do not even find a use for the concept of culture except incidentally when it appears to be a kind of epiphenomenon or gloss emerging from the basic social structure.

The above statements are a greatly simplified résumé of the difference between nineteenth-century evolutionism and the most prevalent and successful kinds of modern study. The point of the résumé is not to epitomize or analyze, however, but merely to stipulate now as a point of departure that the nineteenth-century conception of culture in terms of general stages influenced the study of primitive social organization in one way and allowed certain advances, whereas modern nonevolutionary functionalism, with its interest focused on particular societies, has been influential in another way and has made certain other kinds of advances. If this is so in some general sense, it follows that neither is the only way. What remains to be done is to put them together so that more of the whole story is told, and so that certain problems in the study of primitive social organization may be brought under the kind of scrutiny that neither of the above views can do alone.

Evolutionary interests have been reviving in America, and at midcentury three books on evolution have had some important things to say about social organization. These are J. H. Steward's *Theory of Culture Change* (1955), W. Goldschmidt's *Man's Way* (1959), and L. A. White's *The Evolution of Culture* (1959). The present work, similar to these three in some ways, differs from them in important respects.

It is, first of all, concerned more directly with major problems in the study of social organization than with a general treatment of all aspects of culture. Second, the conception of evolution used is one which weds nineteenth-century evolutionism to modern theory in the terms described in Sahlins and Service's *Evolution and Culture* (1960). Third, and perhaps most important, this book uses new or different perspectives and concepts which seem theoretically congenial to the above evolutionary theory but which nevertheless have not been consistently used before.

SOME ASPECTS OF THE EVOLUTIONARY PERSPECTIVE

The word "evolution" has had two meanings. In the usual perspective of American biologists, evolution is phylogenetic; the interest is in the historical sequence of adaptive changes in related forms. There is also a different perspective on evolution which is concerned with progress as such, with the rise of higher forms. Progress is measured by some absolute criterion, such as complexity of structure or level of integration, and the forms are classified in broad overall stages. The taxonomy used is not phylogenetic, for the concern is not with the historic or genetic relationship of the diverse forms, but rather with their structural-functional differences in order of appearance, no matter what their relationship or the line of descent to which they pertain. This view, which is descended from nineteenth-century interests, has been called "General Evolution" by Sahlins in order to distinguish it from the perspective concerned with adaptive changes in particular lines, or "Specific Evolution" (Sahlins and Service, 1960). In the following chapters the broad classification of types of social organization will be made in terms of stages in general evolution. The movement from one stage to another, however, is viewed in terms of specific advance. It should be emphasized that these are not two separate kinds of evolution but rather two perspectives, two contexts into which the same data can be placed for different intellectual purposes.

Adaptation in Evolution

Environmental adaptation, cultural ecology, and other similar conceptions have been frequently used in cultural anthropology. In the evolutionary context, however, adaptation should have a somewhat broader significance than it is usually given. Adaptation to *habitat, environment,* or *ecology* seems to have been restricted to the relationship of a culture or society to the natural environment alone. In biology, however, adaptation refers to all aspects of the universe that impinge on the breeding population. Thus a biological population has symbiotic, parasitic, or competitive relationships to other populations. In anthropological studies, when there is concern with the adaptation of any particular culture, other societies are not usually considered. *Acculturation, revivalistic movements, colonialism,* and other such concepts are used when the concern is with the relations between cultures. But in the view taken here, all of these responses, and others, will be seen as kinds of adaptive processes, in addition to the adjustments made to the noncultural habitat. This view of adaptation helps solve some problems and also, of course, brings up new ones. (See Goldschmidt [1959, pp. 119–132]; Harding, in Sahlins and Service [1960, Ch. 3]; and Lesser [1961] for further explication.)

Our Contemporary Ancestors

There has long been an injunction in anthropology against using data from contemporary primitive cultures to characterize ancient cultural forms. "Their history is as long as ours," goes the argument that is supposed to make this an unwarranted procedure. The rebuttal to this is not, of course, "No, it isn't: it's shorter." Certainly aboriginal Arunta culture is not younger than Western civilization; it is obviously a great deal older, and precisely therein lies one of the virtues of studying that kind of culture. There also has been a related sort of injunction: anthropologists ought to stop calling such cultures "primitive," "simple," or "preliterate" (Herskovits, 1955, pp. 358–363).

But if the aboriginal culture of the Arunta of Australia is not a form of adaptation to a particular kind of (total) environment made long, long ago and preserved into modern times because of its isolation, then what is it? Does a people have whatever kind of culture it might dream up at any given time? Obviously not. Do the Arunta have a rudimentary technology and simple social life because that is as far as their mental powers would take them? No. Anthropologists would deny that these people have such a limited mental capacity. What else can explain such a culture, then, but that there have been survivals into the present of ancient cultural forms which because of relative isolation have maintained a relatively stable adaptation. Many primitive societies have changed greatly in modern times and ultimately all will be changed, assimilated, or obliterated, but that only makes the point more clear. Where an Arunta-like way of life is not yet significantly altered by modern influences it is a culture that is primitive, ancient, and preliterate. And it has a very long history, too, for the Arunta culture is paleolithic in *type*, although the paleolithic *era* ended when and where higher stages arose—a long time ago. (E. B. Tylor [1894] made many of the above points with reference to the Tasmanians.)

Thus the study of the cultures of various primitive societies should have great utility not only for testing the variety of human cultural responses and making controlled comparisons, but also for collecting useful facts with which to

think more realistically about past stages of cultural evolution. In this sense anthropology possesses a time machine.
However, this figure of speech should not suggest that data
from modern primitive cultures can be used in some mechanical, simple-minded fashion. The historical situation
that led to the discovery of primitive peoples and made them
scientifically observable is the very situation that began to
alter them. In fact, many contemporary primitive cultures
began adapting to civilization in one way or another long
before they were studied by trained anthropologists. To
simply make a count of modern primitive societies without
considering the kind of adaptation to aspects of modern
civilization leads to nothing but confusion, no matter how
refined the statistical techniques used. For example, a large
number of the societies included in the Human Relations
Area Files do not have an aboriginal social organization;
many have, in fact, the organization, or lack of organization,
of a displaced persons' camp.[1] Therefore, in thinking about
the paleolithic or neolithic eras in terms of ethnographic
data, one must use judgment; some of the cultures are much
more relevant and useful than others and some are not
relevant at all.

The attempt here will be first to discuss the social life
of the various stages and eras of cultural evolution in terms
of relevant data from aboriginal societies. Consideration
will also be given to some of the ethnologically well-known
groups which have acquired their social characteristics in
modern times. We should be interested in various social
forms no matter what they are adapted to—because they
do exist and have been studied—but it seems probable that

---

[1] Such *composite* groups of disorganized, decimated refugees probably
existed during all historical epochs, but they must have been rare and
sporadic compared to their modern counterparts created by the whole-
sale, widespread, and nearly simultaneous devastation wrought on the
primitive world by the expansion of civilization.

the analysis of many problems in the study of primitive social life is advanced by keeping in mind the differences between the aboriginal kinds of organization and those adapted to modern conditions.

Speculation About Origins

Many modern American anthropologists have said that you shouldn't "speculate about origins" and many British anthropologists, especially Radcliffe-Brown, have denounced "conjectural history."

This book is rife with speculation and conjecture. Scientists in other fields follow this procedure frequently and are not criticized for it. It must be admitted, however, that there is danger when either the reader or the writer is so foolish as to mistake the speculations for truths. The anthropologists who warn against speculation seem to have had in mind some of the bitter arguments between adherents of "schools of thought," such as those who believed in Morgan's theory that early human society was sexually promiscuous, or who upheld Maine's patriarchal theory, or McLennan's marriage-by-capture theory. The error, however, lay in the nonscientific, clannish antagonisms which turned speculations into convictions. But the way to cope with such human frailties is not to foreswear or outlaw theory, speculations, and conjectures, for they are an important part of scientific thought. Rather, there must be an effort to be wary of the emotional states and social or political circumstances that transform mere speculations such as the *Kon Tiki* notions into vehemently held beliefs, for then they resemble religion rather than science. As scientists we should not take our firmest stand over the thinnest ice, even though this seems to be a normal human trait.

WHAT IS SOCIAL ORGANIZATION?

The most important and general of the perspectives that needs reconsideration for an evolutionary analysis involves the very definition of social organization and social structure. Winick's *Dictionary of Anthropology* (1956) defines *structure, social* (there is no entry for "social organization") as "the ordered relation which the parts of a society have to each other, seen from a reasonably long-range point of view." This is a conception of social structure or social organization—and, for that matter, of kinship organization—which appears to be congenial to a number of anthropologists, though not to all. Winick goes on to say: "Anthropological viewpoints of social structure have ranged from seeing it as a web of all the interpersonal relations in a community to the relations among only the major groups."

The extremes among the various conceptions seem to be related to a concern with the relationship and integration of groups of the society as opposed to an interest in interpersonal conduct alone. Not all anthropologists take one side to the exclusion of the other, however. Walter Goldschmidt says: "The structure of a society involves two things: first, there is a division into smaller social units, which we call groups; and second, there are recognized social positions (statuses) and appropriate behavior patterns to such positions (roles)" (1960, p. 266). Goldschmidt's emphasis on distinguishing *statuses* and their special functions and relations from *groups* and their functions and relations is so thoroughgoing that in his book of readings, *Exploring the Ways of Mankind,* the essays dealing with status are in one section of the book (subtitled "The Relationships among Men"), and essays dealing with the family and other groups in society are in another section.

Inasmuch as the most important, formidable, and long-standing problems in studies of kinship and social organization have to do with the relationship, lack of relationship, or degree or kind of relationship between the configuration of society in its integration of groups, on the one hand, and the nature of the status network on the other, it is necessary to distinguish clearly the one from the other in the very beginning. We shall, therefore, accept Goldschmidt's dichotomy. "Social structure" hereafter will refer to the component groups of a society and to the configuration of their arrangement. The network of statuses, however, will be regarded as a different order of things. Statuses are named social positions which are assigned conventional attributes and roles that regulate or influence the conduct of interpersonal relations. They are commonly such social positions as kinship relationships and classes or categories of persons based on marital state, sex, age, occupation, and so on, when these positions have to do with roles in social interaction. "Social organization" will be retained as in general and vague usage to refer to the totality of both structure and statuses.

Groups

If social structure refers to groups and to the character of their total configuration or articulation then it would seem to be a simple matter to delineate various social structures, compare them, and discuss their probable development. It is not simple, however, largely because of some semantic problems. In the effort to make analysis of social structure easier these problems need to be discussed and resolved.

There are several kinds of things that have been called groups and they have been defined variously by sociologists and anthropologists for different analytical purposes. Tönnies' famous distinction between *Gemeinshaft* and *Gesellschaft*, translated usually as "communal" and "associative" groups, was the starting point for most of the various conceptions. Some students have emphasized the difference between familistic or kin groups and nonfamilistic groups; others distinguish groups with volitional as opposed to ascribed membership; some contrast coresidential, or spatial, or territorial groups to special-purpose groups. All of these distinctions are suggestive and useful, but for the main problems to be faced in this book the matter of coresidence is the crucial one.

The present conception of social structure includes such groups as (a) domestic families or households, lineage villages, and territorial bands, which are relatively permanent aggregations of people, and (b) such cross-cutting, dispersed associations as clans, secret societies, clubs, and so on, which help tie them together and articulate them. These are obviously not the same kind of things. For example, it will appear later that for certain purposes it is necessary to distinguish clearly between a local lineage and a clan, which is nonlocal. Both are familistic, based on kinship ties of a sort, and both are of ascribed membership. They are different in that one is spatial, local, territorial, and coresidential, whereas the other is not. Because the group is based importantly on a large measure of propinquity and continuity, the terms "spatial," "local," or "territorial" are not quite suggestive enough for such groups as the domestic family, a lineage, a neighborhood, or a village. Let us call such groups *residential* (the "co-" seems unnecessary).

A residential group *exists,* and its reasons for existing are complicated: it exists where certain people live for economic reasons, for political reasons, for biological reasons, and perhaps still others. Sheer propinquity through time, created by whatever congeries of factors, is the important basis of the sociality. The point is that the group seems *natural* (though the use of that word brings up difficulties) and therefore does not have to have such strong cultural buttressing and special appurtenances as does, say, a secret society, clan, or scout troop. This latter type, the nonresidential, may or may not have a single special purpose, may or may not be familistic, or ascribed, or exclusive.

Robert Lowie (1948, p. 14) pondered the naming problem of nonresidential groups and found "corporation," "society," and such words to be too ambiguous because of their alternative usages. He suggested instead the word "sodality," from the Latin *sodalis,* to refer to voluntary associations as opposed to kinship and residence groups. We must alter this meaning somewhat, however, because a nonlocal clan, for example, is *not* voluntary and *is* based on kinship, yet such an organization as a clan is one that we want to distinguish from a residential group. Let us use sodality to mean, simply, a nonresidential association that has some corporate functions or purposes. Thus sodality is close in spirit to *Gesellshaft* and "special-purpose group," but it has the advantage of not implying either voluntary membership or, necessarily, a *single* special purpose and thus is a somewhat broader concept, and it is explicitly defined as nonresidential whereas the others are nonresidential only by implication or expectation.

Because a family or a neighborhood is a residential unit it does not have the same kind of origin as a clan, club, or college of priests. It also looks and acts different. It is there; you can see it. Its quality is that it is truly a group, an agglomeration. On the other hand, it could be argued that sodalities are not groups at all for they are never consistently or even necessarily frequently agglomerated. For this reason cultural inventions such as a name, ceremony, mythology, insignia of membership, and so on are so much more common in sodalities than in face-to-face residential groups —they are much more necessary. It follows that some residential groups are relatively dispersed, or in the case of nations so large, that they approach being sodalities in some measure and take on many of the cultural characteristics of sodalities—for example, the use of flags, anthems, mythology, and ceremony in order to make membership more meaningful.

The main point, however, is that residential groups and sodalities have different origins and courses of development. Residential groups, and the changes in them, are essentially demographic matters. Sodalities are not directly demographic and respond differently to increases in population or density or numbers of residential groups. Another important thing about sodalities is that, being nonlocal, they come to have political functions by cross-cutting, and thus integrating, different residential units. It is mainly in this sense that sodalities should be included in the conception of social structure. They are not groups exactly, but they have an important relationship to the true groups, the residential units; they are important grouplike means of integrating residential groups and arranging the configuration of the society.

The political integrating effect of sodalities brings up the matter of function. It does not necessarily, or even frequently, follow that the human inventiveness or intent so characteristic in the rise of sodalities is directed to the end, or purpose, of causing greater political integration. But any sodality, even such a peculiar, limited, and nonpolitical one as The Society for the Preservation of Barbershop Quartet Singing, can be a unity of sorts which cross-cuts some proportion, however small, of the residential groups and thus plays some role in integrating the society. It is apparent that we must contrast what is sometimes called latent function with manifest function or, if you like, sociological function with purpose. Any sodality, of whatever kind and whatever purpose, will have an integrating sociological or latent function just because it is nonresidential, and some kinds in some circumstances will perform this function more importantly than others, no matter what their manifest purposes might be.

Function is, of course, related to structure. Yet the relationship may be direct and simple or indirect and complex. Sodalities have one or a few manifest functions or purposes which are normally directly and even obviously related to their structure; the structure is, in a real sense, created by the manifest function—to *do* the function. Latent functions, however, such as the cross-cutting or integrating effects, are incidental and implicit social by-products of the structure, however important. Residential groups, on the other hand, have a structure which is largely unrelated to their manifest function. A domestic family has manifest functions such as childrearing and economic cooperation, but the actual structure of the family is a complex consequence of biology, ecology, economy, and cultural modes such as marriage customs. It may be virilocal or uxorilocal, polygamous or monogamous, extended or nuclear, large or small, urban or rural. It can function somehow in rearing and educating children and as an economic unit in any of these cases—sometimes almost in spite of its structure. Because of the different relations of structure to function of residential groups as opposed to sodalities, we can see their origin and course of development and general role in social organization as distinct, and for that reason the two kinds of things must be kept conceptually separated when evolutionary problems are addressed.

Statuses

Although statuses presuppose a social structure, they do not always or necessarily correspond to any particular group of persons, an agglomeration locatable in space, or to a sodality. Female and male statuses, for example, do not usually comprise two separate residential groups; most groups, in fact, include both. The statuses of female and male are classifications of persons made in terms of certain characteristics, ascribed and inherent, and they are assigned different roles no matter where the persons are located.

There are times, to be sure, when a status is given to a particular group, as to a Royal Family, but the point is that there is no *necessary* connection between a status and a group. That a group may sometimes also have a status is no reason for confusing the two concepts. The important feature of statuses is that the context of their function is interpersonal conduct and only this.

A similar distinction can be made between statuses and sodalities. Membership in a particular sodality may confer a status or it may not. Also, a particular status may be a prerequisite to membership in a sodality, or it may not. One must be a woman to be a member of the League of Women Voters, yet not all women are members. But in some societies all unmarried males in a small community are automatically members of a Men's Club or Warrior Society, so that status and the sodality are coterminous in these cases. That sometimes there is a direct relationship between groups and status and sodalities and status and sometimes there is not, and that sometimes statuses are not related to either, are reasons for the conceptual distinction. In this way we are better able to find out what the relationship is, if any, in particular cases, and trace variations in the relationship in the course of evolutionary change.

It is necessary, too, to make an explicit definition of kinship statuses. As implied above, kinship terms normally label kinds of statuses; they are familistic and egocentric status terms. They are not simply labels for the parts and groups of the society, but are the names or titles referring to social positions that determine forms of interpersonal conduct. As mentioned earlier, many modern anthropologists still seem to think with Morgan that kinship terminologies are "systems of consanguinity and affinity," that they give a picture of the genealogical makeup of the society. This view is exemplified in the definition given in Winick's *Dictionary of Anthropology*: "*Kinship;* the social recognition and expression of genealogical relationships, both con-

sanguinal and affinal." This lingering, perhaps unconsciously held, assumption about kinship terms has confused
and impeded our understanding of many important problems. Is it not obvious that if kinship terminologies did in
fact express the familistic social structure then there would
be no problems about the relationship of the two? Yet that
relationship has been a basic and continuing source of argument in anthropology from its beginning up to today.

If kinship terms are thought of as kinds of status terms,
the problem of the relationship of terminologies to social
structure is clarified considerably. Status terms are related
to certain aspects of social structure, but not to all. A genealogical position may be a status position, but not all genealogical positions are; membership in certain groups and
sodalities may confer a status term, but not all groups and
sodalities have such a characteristic; being a member of a
category of persons such as married or unmarried, strong or
weak, bright or stupid, comical or grave, brave or cowardly,
skilled or unskilled, also may or may not confer a named
status. What a person *is* for purposes of social conduct,
etiquette, or role, consists of a great many possible attributes.
Those selected as relevant to status positions, however, must
be much fewer, but they are variable from one social context to another and enormously so from one kind of society
to another. To say that some status terms are *related* to
social structure is not to say that the relationship is simple
or invariable; above all, it does not follow that a given pattern of status nomenclature *reflects* or *gives a picture of* the
society. How much it does so and in what ways still needs
discussion.

A SHORT GLOSSARY OF SOCIAL RULES

It is appropriate now to make more explicit descriptions
and definitions of certain of the most important ideological

determinants of social behavior, inasmuch as there is no
standard usage for them. They are here called *rules*, using
the Random House Dictionary's common first meaning:
"A principle or regulation governing conduct, action, procedure, arrangement, etc."

Marital Residence Rules[2]

These are usually called "postmarital residence rules," but
the "post-" seems redundant, if not wrong ("after" a state
of marriage must mean a divorced state in a literal sense).

Virilocal marital residence will mean, in accordance with
fairly prevalent modern usage, that the married couple
customarily becomes part of the male's natal residence
group.

Uxorilocal marital residence will mean that the couple
customarily becomes part of the female's natal group.

Patrilocal and *matrilocal,* rather than the terms above,
have frequently been used for the two basic marital residence rules, but these words signify better the modal consequences of those rules. When virilocal residence is consistent the children of the union are born into and grow up
in father's own group; with uxorilocal residence they are
born and raised in mother's own group. Hence the words
"patrilocal" and "matrilocal" will be used from now on to
refer to the composition of the group and not to the marital
residence rule. Thus a patrilocal band presupposes virilocal
residence, yet because it is desirable to keep names of groups
distinct from names of rules, these words will not be regarded as synonymous. A further reason for this usage is
that we should not confuse a group formed by a residence
mode with a true descent group.

---

[2] Following Adam (1947).

Descent Reckoning

Here again, but with greater complexity, it becomes necessary to define some terms in order to keep the names of conceptual things distinct from names for the composition of groups. Descent reckoning is a conceptual means by which a people can describe the vertical, generational, relationships of persons to each other, the makeup of certain residential groups and sodalities, and perhaps the interrelations of all of these. This can be done *nonlineally* or *cognatically* (through any relatives) and *lineally* (patrilineally or matrilineally, in the normal sense of those words). There is no difficulty, nor departure from current usage (except for dropping "uni" from the redundant, but commonly used, "unilineal"), but we must be clear as to what is *not* descent reckoning and particularly what the reckoning has to do with groups.

A *descent group,* in the terms proposed here, is one which is understood by the people themselves as being composed of descendants of a common ancestor or pair. It can be lineal—members related in only a patrilineal or only a matrilineal way—or nonlineal (cognatic). But it is important to distinguish these kinds that are conceptualized by a true recognition of descent from those that de facto may be composed of such relatives without their knowing it. In band society generally, and in some tribal societies, for example, groups may be composed of people related through a line of males because of a virilocal marital residence rule. This we may call a *patrilocal* group, as distinguished from a *patrilineal* group by the absence of descent reckoning. In such groups the way in which relationships are calculated and statuses created are by lateral (or horizontal) calculations—people lie in degrees of distance *out* from a point (person, place, or group). In true descent reckoning the calculation is vertical; a contemporary relative is far or distant, of such and such a degree of relationship, depending on how many generations *up* (or past) the collateral departure from Ego's line was made. Status terminologies in such societies, as well as the internal structure of the descent group itself, are different, and are later in evolutionary development.

It is also necessary to distinguish a *common-descent group* from the above. A common-descent group is a sort of half-way house between a local group formed merely by marital residence rules and one which is characterized by full descent reckoning of the relationship of its members. The common-descent group is one which recognizes the fact of common ancestry from a founder or pair, but does not thereafter distinguish lines of descent or differentiation of members by degrees of relationship to the main line of descendants. The relationship of contemporaneous members of the group is in terms of various considerations (to be detailed later) that are lateral rather than vertical.

In all of these, so far, it has been emphasized that our attention is on the conceptualized recognition of descent, in whatever form, by the members of the society. This is necessary in order to avoid the confusion that has been created in some anthropological discussions of kinship by the use of the term "descent line" when the recognition of its existence is by the anthropologist, not the people involved. This is a kind of semantic knot particularly characteristic of some of the arguments made about Australian kinship. At this point it is necessary only to make clear that descent lines invented by anthropologists will not be regarded in this book as descent lines.[3]

The present conception of descent also excludes inheritance, succession, and affiliation. Inheritance and succession need include only the passage of goods, a name, a status,

---

[3] E. R. Leach (1951) has shown how the failure to distinguish local groups from implicit descent lines has confused analyses of certain Australian societies made by Murdock and Lévi-Strauss.

a membership, etc., between two persons, as from father to child, mother to child, father to son, mother to daughter, and so on. Many of us have often confused patrilineal descent with father-child inheritance and/or succession, matrilineal descent with mother-child inheritance and/or succession, and even patrilineal or matrilineal descent with father-son, mother-daughter inheritance-succession. (These latter are parallel by sex; they are not patrilineal or matrilineal, and they are not *descent* in the definitions to be used here.)

We have been particularly confused by mixing descent with affiliation.[4] Any true descent group—say, a patrilineal group—must also have a certain rule of affiliation to it, in this case from father to children. Hence, it is easy to see these terms as self-reciprocal or synonymous. But the converse is not true; affiliation in some groups may be father-to-child, but the group need not necessarily be patrilineal, nor even a descent group. It may be, and frequently is, merely a patrilocal band, which is not the same thing. In fact, it is possible to have membership ascribed in these ways to a group or sodality which is not composed of relatives at all. Sons may conventionally follow fathers to a certain prep school or to a Hopi curing society, but it does not follow that the contemporaneous members are related to each other. Inheritance, succession, and affiliation, it may be apparent, refer to rules having to do with individuals; they are related to structure and status in important ways but are not *themselves* either structure or status. For this reason it is desirable to distinguish them.

---

[4] See similar arguments by Scheffler (1968, p. 543) and Schneider (1967).

2

In the Beginning

Man is a vertebrate, mammalian, and primate animal. That is what man *is,* and the fact should never be lost from account. Yet there is something peculiar about man. The usual way of stating it is to say that man has culture, or that he has symbolic communication which results in culture. These are ways of saying that man himself has somehow added to the purely biological and situational determinants of his behavior certain others of his own invention which have increasingly involved his individual self-interests in a simultaneous commitment to his fellows. This is not always nor exclusively the case, of course, for man is still an animal, but so often and so strikingly is it so that much of philosophy and religion as well as several sciences have been concerned with the unique aspects of man's behavior rather than with the biological continuities which ally him with the other primates.

The difficult subject at hand now is to discuss, or speculate about, the continuities and discontinuities of the man-primate relationship in the most pertinent context, the origin of human social culture. It is not *mere* speculation to do this, however, for there is information about primate social life, about early man in the archaeological record, and about early types of society retained by some ethnographically known hunting-gathering bands. These items, however sparse, can be used to temper the speculation.

The phrase "human culture" is redundant. Culture is human and only human. It depends on an as yet inadequately defined mental capacity of human beings to communicate with each other and, correlatively, to think imaginatively in ways that apparently no other animal can. Other animals communicate and "think" but in no case can it be shown that they relate future times, other places, and even nonexistent things and places with each other. This mental gymnastic has been called the "symbolic capacity" by the ethnologist L. A. White (1949) and has been discussed in other ways by linguists (as grammar, for example, by Greenberg, 1959) and by philosophers (especially Cassirer, 1944). For the present purpose, the salient feature of man's symbolic capacity is that with it he socially creates determinants of his own behavior; that is, he invents and communicates cultural rules and values which influence his social life. This is the point at which certain subhuman abilities and propensities are emphasized, submerged, or altered, and discontinuities between subhuman primate and human behavior arise.

It sounds paradoxical, or perhaps illogical,[1] to describe culture as a determinant of the behavior of the very species that created it. But if we distinguish between the origin of a trait and its later symbolic existence as a part of an ongoing cultural tradition, then we can speak of it in this latter phase as constituting a determining factor (among others) in the behavior of every new member born into the society. It is a part of the "social heritage." Thus the statements "Man creates culture" and "Culture creates man" may be equally apposite, though opposite, generalizations.

---

[1] As it does to Bidney (1953, Ch. II).

PRIMATE SOCIALITY

Society is coextensive with life; and aside from that total
"web of life" interrelationship, all living things participate
in some form of more intimate social life that is peculiar to
their species. The diversity in kinds of specific social organization is enormous; among the primates alone there are
grand differences from one species to another. It is therefore
difficult to speculate about the social life of man's primate
ancestors from evidence derived from studies of modern
primates except in very gross generalities. These are well
known and therefore will be mentioned only briefly.

All primates, and man particularly, have a prolonged
infantile period of dependence and tutelage in relationship
with the mother. This biological factor is probably the basis
for such emotions as "love" and the "need for positive affect" (Goldschmidt, 1959, pp. 26–29), and for the acceptance
of submissive roles. We should also note at this point that
the mother-child relationship is the first and by far the most
invariable of the dyadic, pairing, relationships that become
elements in the later human family.[2]

Prolonged immaturity among primates also tends to result in the coexistence of individuals of different ages in the
highly sociable play groups. Such circumstances result in the
socialization of those individuals in terms of varying dominant and submissive social roles outside the mother-child
relationship.

The above characteristics of primates is in the end a result
of primate biological traits. But why should there be groups
at all, except for the mother-child dyad? This question has
been discussed at length by White (1959, Chs. 3 and 4) who
follows Zuckerman (1932) in relating forms of primate social

---

[2] See R. N. Adams (1960) for a discussion of the significance of dyads
in analyzing family types.

organization to the search for mates, food, and protection. It will be convenient to discuss primate group life in these terms, although the opinions put forward will be somewhat different from those of Zuckerman and White. From the point of view of an individual, be he man or marmot, there are assuredly these three basic needs. From the point of view of selective pressures in the adaptation of a society, however, these three needs are involved in very different ways, and in different proportions.

The use of the word "search" with respect to these three factors suggests that they are all things outside the group which operate as selective factors in determining the character of the group. But whereas kinds of food and variations in its supply and the presence or absence of predators and competitors may be readily seen as possible selective factors, sex is not this sort of thing. The sexual behavior of a species is biological and a constant for the species. Sex, therefore, should be discussed in the same context as other individual biological features, like prolonged immaturity, rather than as a variable environmental factor which selects for certain traits.

But of course the biological traits of primates that made group life possible in the first place may well have undergone considerable elaboration as environmental conditions continued to favor group life. This is to say that the degree of affection, intelligence, need for positive affect, and so on, that modern primates exhibit was probably selected for in nature as group life continued to be advantageous.

The relation of sex to the formation of social groups has been studied and discussed in terms of breeding seasonality. Some species of animals form families and/or herds only during a rutting season and are dispersed (except for the mother-offspring dyads) the rest of the time. Primate groups, on the other hand, tend to be year-round associations and it has been assumed that this permanence is *caused* by the lack of clear-cut seasonality in sex urges. Some doubt has

been cast on this assumption by modern specialists (Imanishi, 1960, pp. 394–399; Chance, in Imanishi, p. 404;
Washburn, *et al.,* 1965; Jay, 1968). Thus, while male-female
dyads among primates can be thought of as primarily sexual,
the important question of why groups which include *several
adult males* are formed apparently requires consideration
of nonbiological or situational factors. At this point we may
more appropriately discuss food and protection.

Food supplies, their kind, amount, seasonal prevalence,
and so on can obviously affect demography. Upper limits
in population size and density are of course established by
the amounts of food available, though it does not follow that
a society always, or even frequently, grows to or remains at
the size that is potentially possible. But to say that food
supplies establish demographic limits is not to say anything
about why primate groups are formed in the first place.

The amount of predation to which primates have been
subjected, as well as the amount of intraspecies conflict,
must have been enormously variable from time to time,
place to place, and species to species. Yet it would require
no great stretch of imagination to accept that there was
probably some predation much of the time—enough, at
any rate, to operate as an environmental selective factor
over a very long period. This must have been particularly
true of the environment of proto-man, who was undoubtedly a ground-dweller.[3] It might be added, also, that
the closer the primate species resembled man the more
dangerous the intraspecies conflict would become, man
being the most dangerous animal of all.

It seems clear from modern studies of primates that the
protection provided by group life is of great importance.
As Washburn (1960a, p. 4) remarks of baboons: "The troop
is the survival mechanism. To not be a social animal is to

---

[3] Washburn (1957) states that the Australopithecines were probably
preyed upon by other animals.

be a dead animal." DeVore concludes that "A basic function of male dominance in a primate social system may well be protection—both from predators and from territorial encroachment by an adjoining group" (Ms. quoted in Clark, 1960, p. 313). Other observers have emphasized how the long period of dependency of juveniles involves not only nutrition but their protection.

THE BEGINNINGS OF CULTURAL SOCIALITY

The acquisition of culture depended on a development of the primate brain to the point which made possible the use of symbols in communication and thought. With symbols humans can plan ways to cooperate and create means to enhance and perpetuate the cooperative relationship. There is, of course, some prehuman basis for sharing and cooperation; it exists variously in such situations as the rearing of the young, collective defense, grooming behavior, and most obvious of all, sexual activity.

Such sporadic, ephemeral, and situational approximations to collaboration could have served as models or lessons for early man. Once symbolic thought and communication become possible new determinants of behavior can be invented on the basis of evidence or knowledge which is already present. Sanctions, rules, proscriptions, and values can be created and established which inhibit conflict and strengthen solidarity. Thus sharing can be changed from mere situational expediency to a norm and a *good* thing, with positive social rewards when it is done and social punishments when it is not done. The few forms of social dependence found in ape society could, by cultural means, be greatly extended and intensified. Data from all known human groups attest to the enormous importance of sharing as a means of creating friends and allies or of strengthening existing amiable relationships. The more primitive the society and the more straitened the circumstances, the greater the emphasis on sharing, and the more scarce or needed the items the greater the sociability engendered.

All that was necessary, then, was the symbolic ability to make some rules and values which would extend, intensify, and regularize tendencies which already existed. Sharing creates dependencies and alliances; seizing food or mates by force or threat creates enemies. The advantages of reciprocal sharing must have been readily apparent, but even if they were not, those persons with the largest number of allies or with the firmest alliances must have been enormously aided in the struggle for existence. Thus sharing conferred great selective advantage in adaptation, whether we think of the survival of whole groups or of individuals.

A simple act of sharing-out, of giving, is not of itself necessarily symbolic or cultural. Sharing-out with the understanding of a return, however, involves the concept of reciprocity at *another time*. Such an understanding, perforce, depends on symbolic communication. In fact it involves the very essence of the symbol, for symbolic thought, and only symbolic thought, makes it possible to imagine (as well as talk about) things not present or things to be done in the future.

So far the action has been discussed as though it were the consequence of individual realizations of the immediate usefulness, both practical and social, of a reciprocal agreement. We seem to be talking about an individual's self-interest alone, rather than about his commitment to his society; or, to put it another way, we are talking about individual intentions rather than sociological functions. But how and in what ways, we may wonder, is *society* involved in reciprocity? How is reciprocity made into cultural activity characteristic of a group? There is no answer, nor conclusive argument, possible. Only a modest reasonableness can be introduced at this point by arguing for a logical principle. It would seem that the most likely origin of a culture trait which is a prescription or proscription of social consequence would be when *short-term results* of an action also have important *long-term results*. When obvious individual self-interest is served (typically a relatively short-term perspective) which subsequently coincides with an advantage to others or perhaps even to the whole group (a longer-term perspective), then it is likely to become more permanently sanctioned and thus more of a sociological factor. The actions of separate individuals in reciprocal giving, which confer such obvious social advantages to the partners of the exchange, may be assumed to be precisely those which finally are sanctioned as more general cultural rules and values.

It seems logical to assume that as a basis for later developments the most significant of the early rules of reciprocity was related to the acquiescence of two social groups in the reciprocal giving of females. The sharing of females was not necessarily the *first* instance of human reciprocity and cooperation; the sharing of food, collaboration in the hunt and in fighting, or giving help in any number of exigencies conceivably could have antedated the giving of mates. But all of those would have been sporadic and dependent on varying circumstances, so that it would be the conception of reciprocal sharing only in a general sense that would be sanctioned at first. The "search for mates," however, differs from the above in being more continuous as well as more consistently important, so that a general rule of sharing could give rise to a more particular kind of sharing, the sharing of females. And the reciprocity involved would also be an easier kind to institute in the sense that it would involve less of a generalized *trust* and a more specifically designated understanding—a female for a female.

Reciprocity between families or groups is what turns mere mating into marriage, for it involves the assumption of some stability or relative permanency in the pairing arrangement. Because groups have agreed on it, the two actual partners have less choice and less freedom to change the arrangement than would be the case if their own fickle and promiscuous urges alone were being satisfied.

Marriage becomes a more stable pairing arrangement, too, when the sexual division of labor is regularized. The freedom of males to range more widely in the hunt than females, as noted above, may have been a factor in this development. From the point of view of cooperation in the hunt, which under early conditions of simple technology must have been very important, a team of males can continuously range together widely whereas at any given time certain females cannot, which prejudices teamwork.

Marriage, then, from the point of view of the individuals involved in it, came to confer positive economic advantages as the division of labor became more specialized. Men hunt and fight, women gather vegetable food, cook, and bear and care for children. Each is better off (economically) married than single. This situation may have been responsible for the fact that hunting-gathering societies are more standardly monogamous than are others. But the advantages of marriage rules to the society at large are of great consequence, too. The most significant and general aspect of these, from the societal point of view, is *exogamy:* one marries outside some defined social group. Concomitant with this is *endogamy:* one does not marry too far out. Probably the early rule referred to marriage into a specific other group, and thus simultaneously had its exogamic and endogamic implications.

Exogamic rules of marriage serve two obvious functions: (a) out-marriage reduces the probability of jealous conflict among males within the group; (b) it forms alliances and dependencies between the groups which supply the partners. Some anthropologists emphasize the first, the resolution of intrasocietal conflict, whereas others emphasize intergroup reciprocity. Both are important, but it would seem that the earliest and most significant was the intergroup aspect in which the short-term and obvious aims of security serve also for long-term adaptive advantage, for both individuals and whole groups. That it would consequently lead to smoother relations within a group and thus confer ultimately some selective advantage in that respect would seem to have been a fortuitous social by-product of marriage customs and not related to their origin. Prehuman primate groups were already ordered internally in a hierarchy of dominance statuses; it was the relations between groups that were dangerous and unordered. Offense-defense requirements, rather than food and sex needs, thus appear again as the most important determinants of the first cultural—purposeful—orderings. The advantages of reciprocal out-marriages must have been "plainly before their minds." [4]

At this point it should be noted that the above conception is somewhat different from the most prevalent and long-standing interpretations of early human social organization. Most nineteenth-century evolutionists gave the prohibition of incest great prominence as the first cultural regulation of sex in the interest of society, possibly because of its apparent universality in human society. Also, in many instances the incest taboo was seen as related to exogamy, as though they were negative and positive phrasings of the same rule. There is a logical basis for disagreement with both of these ideas.

First we should consider the fact that exogamy refers to *marriage*, whereas the incest rule is a prohibition of *sexual intercourse* within a defined group of close relatives. These

---

[4] E. B. Tylor (1888) made this point long ago.

Among tribes of low culture there is but one means known of keeping up permanent alliance, and that means is intermarriage. . . . Again and again in the world's history, savage tribes must have had plainly before their minds the simple practical alternative between marrying-out and being killed-out. Even far on in culture, the political value of intermarriage remains. . . . "Then we will give our daughters unto you, and we will take your daughters to us, and we will dwell with you, and we will become one people," is a well-known passage of Israelite history [p. 267].

are obviously not the same kind of thing, hence the two
rules are not simply obverse to each other. There is probably a relationship between them, a functional concomi-
tance perhaps, as will be argued below, but they are not
positive and negative aspects of the same rule.

Equally important, and implicit in the above, is the fact
that exogamic marriage rules refer to relationships *between*
(or among) groups, whereas the incest taboo is a regulation
of individual behavior *within* a group. Again it is apparent
that these are two different kinds of rules and not twin aspects of the same rule.

Primitive marriage, then, takes place between groups and
tends to be reciprocal. It is a particular kind of sharing.
It can be thought of in the context of primitive economics,
for it has the same social results as other kinds of balanced
reciprocal exchanges.

It seems to be that women are the *gifts,* and that the
males' groups are the recipients of the gifts. From the point
of view of the individuals in the marriage each both gives
and receives, of course, but from the societal point of view,
as Lévi-Strauss has emphasized (1949), it is women who are
exchanged. When a man marries a woman there is in one
sense an exchange between two groups at that instant for
each has "given" and the reciprocity is immediately accom-
plished, but none of the hunting-gathering societies ever
see it that way. The female is the gift, the male and his
group the receivers, and the reciprocity is not balanced except by the counter-gift of a female (or of goods sometimes)
from the male's group.

Are women the gifts because, at least in hunting-gathering
societies, a daughter or sister (and subsequently her children) is the most precious thing a family can give? This
may be, for reciprocity is so fundamental a requirement at
low cultural levels that the most precious things are also
those that are given for the most serious social purposes;
also, it seems that the desire for children in such societies

is very great, making a woman more valued for her child-
bearing than she is at higher cultural levels. It is difficult to
judge this proposition, however, for it is overlaid by more
obviously expedient reasons why women and not men appear to be the gifts in hunting-gathering society. The reasons have to do with the tendency toward virilocal marital
residence.[5]

Several possible determinants of virilocality have been
proposed by anthropologists. Some have asserted that it is
a natural result of male dominance. Males do tend to be
dominant in various ways, and that factor may therefore
have something to do with virilocality. It seems inadequate
as an explanation by itself, however, for then how do we
account for composite bands who do not practice any form
of strict marital residence modes? For example, the Chipe-
wayan, the Athabaskan hunters so famous for the dominated
and degraded status of their women, are not ethnographically described as virilocal. Also, it is well known that males
maintain social and political dominance in uxorilocal tribal
societies.

Another reason frequently given for virilocality relates it
to the greater economic importance of males: they are the
hunters and more vital to the group, hence they continue
their residence in it after marriage. But it seems clear that
some bands which depend heavily on woman's work are not
uxorilocal, as would follow from this theory. For example,
the Yahgan of Tierra del Fuego subsist primarily on shellfish, which are gathered only by women.

This economic explanation does lead us in a fruitful di-

---

[5] There is no space here to explain all the reasons for thinking that
virilocal residence was usual in early hunting-gathering society. This
judgment comes from my own research which shows that modern
hunting-gathering bands which are *not* exogamous and virilocal (the
composite bands) are consequences of modern disruption and reconstitution and were not aboriginal. All others, in any environment, were
probably virilocal and exogamous. Chapter 3 discusses this topic more
fully.

rection, however, because it brings our attention to the
sexual division of labor. That men hunt and fight and
women tend children and gather immobile food within a
restricted area could be related to virilocality in two ways.
The first, and the one most frequently suggested, is that
effective hunting requires long residence in the territory.
There are certain difficulties with this notion. One is that
hunters typically range far beyond the band's "country," for
such territories are set principally by the conventional orbit
the band roams in its gathering activities.

But there is a further implication in man's hunting role
which may have significance for the question. Hunting, like
many other male activities such as the conduct of ceremonies,
is often a cooperative enterprise, whereas the activities of
women are ordinarily individualized. Male cooperation is,
of course, most efficiently practiced among men who have
grown up together in the same locality and know each
other's habits and capabilities and who trust each other. *All*
kinds of game are not, of course, hunted cooperatively. Winter sealing by the Eskimo is solitary, as are other kinds of
hunting elsewhere. Yet in all cases, the hunters help each
other find the animals and help bring them home. Perhaps
most important of all, the successful hunter or fisherman
shares with the unsuccessful ones. Strangers presumably
would not share so readily and trustingly as males who grew
up together, and this may well be another important factor
predisposing a group toward virilocality in marriage.

It can be argued, however, that competition among societies could have been the most important cause of virilocality, for if offense-defense requirements are important,
then the trusting cooperation among brothers and other
closely linked male relatives would be more important than
anything else—depending, of course, on the severity of the
competition. Hunting-gathering bands are known to us today usually as peaceful, friendly folk, as suggested in the
book on African Bushmen titled *The Harmless People*

(Thomas, 1959). Nevertheless, the fact that bands are not warlike in modern times does not mean that they never were. Nowadays they are enclaved among more powerful neighbors; most are even subject to police regulation, and they cannot but lose or be heavily punished for any breach of the peace. They are better called "The Helpless People" or "The Defeated People." But one needs only to read a few early accounts of the Australian aborigines, the Fuegians, Athabaskans, Eskimos, or any others before they were so thoroughly subjugated to become convinced that fighting among unrelated groups was one of the main facts of life in aboriginal times. The engagements may have been largely confined to ambushes and other forms of surprise and preventive war, but the small scale of fighting or feuding in no way reduces the degree of fears, dangers, and enmities in those societies which are themselves small. Certainly if fighting was fairly usual the collaboration of male relatives and their close allies in offense-defense must be considered as a significant determinant of social organization. Males, again as in primate society generally, were the "rampart of the troop," hence there was an impulse toward virilocality. A woman, on the other hand, can be lost to her natal band without weakening it.

In a sense, then, a woman is a more "liquid asset" in a band than is a male. In hunting-gathering society the fraternity of males is the unit of most solidarity. And it might be well to reemphasize that cooperation in hunting and offense-defense must have been extraordinarily important when weapons were rudimentary.

SOCIAL STRUCTURE

Early human social structure in its simplest outlines was probably that of a prehuman primate group altered and subdivided in ways directly related to reciprocal, virilocal marriage modes. We cannot know, nor even make a guess, about the size of the proto-human hordes or troops. It is reasonable, however, to assume that they included several females and their offspring and more than one male simply because all primate groups which forage in ecological circumstances similar to those of the Australopithecines are of that sort. All we need posit here is that a number of adults were present.

The analysis does not begin with the nuclear family, or any such "primary group," for those units are best regarded as resultants of the factors being considered. E. W. Count (1958) in a social-biological study of the evolution of sociality concluded as follows:

> In a final survey of the family, we may note: (1) Societies do not take form by a confederation of families, since family is a stable group recognized as such by the society; (2) From its earliest emergence in the vertebrate classes, it has always represented a mood of society, a phase in the biogram of the society; (3) It polarizes but a portion of the society's repertoire of interests; (4) It is shaped by the society much more than it shapes society; that is, its organization fits the institutional demands of society, and it changes if the society changes—it does not initiate societal changes but conforms to them . . . [p. 1080].

The human nuclear family, we may judge, was formed when the total group created the reciprocal marriage rule, making such marriages not occasional (as they must have been for simple short-term individually expedient purposes), but regular between themselves and one or more other groups. The family then crystallized as a relatively stable heterosexual pairing of adults in some consistent association with each other and their offspring.

Another way to say this is that the original primate dyad of mother-offspring, a biological pairing, becomes linked with another, the adult male-female, or conjugal, dyad. It is this latter, of course, which is the most cultural, thus variable in human society, and which therefore should be the focus of investigation in comparative studies of family organization. Many sociologists and anthropologists regard the family as having come into existence *in order to* rear children (because families *do* rear children), and define marriage as a means of legitimatizing the offspring (which it does). Here is another instance of the very different interpretations that come from evolutionary theory as opposed to functionalist theory. In the view taken here, marriage originally had to do with children only incidentally, however important the incident might have been to the children.

This is to say, also, that the social position "father" and its status and role are also secondary. "Husband" must be prior, not only in the temporal sense, but also in that if the most significant early social rule is marriage, "husbandness" and "wifeness" are the first results of it. The father-child dyad is then seen to result from husbandness, that is from the husband's role as provider and protector in the division of labor imposed on the conjugal dyad.

The total exogamous group now became a part-society, inasmuch as some of its former members—its married females—were living in the other group or groups and forms of friendship, alliance, and cooperation now existed among these groups. Within the exogamous groups a nucleus of cooperating males ("brothers") hunted and defended the camp. This, in a sense, was the horizontal solidary unit. The nuclear families formed the vertical solidary units—vertical because each conjugal unit normally begets offspring so that in time this organization bridges two generations and, with luck, three.

This structure also probably had a geographic dimension. Whether the range of habitation was specific or vague, we may assume that the movements of the group were conventionally within a certain "country." Among most ethnologically known hunting-gathering peoples this is so, and, in fact, the name of the band is ordinarily the same as that of the locality it frequents. In accordance with anthropological

precedent we may call this a *local band*. This is not to say
that strict boundaries were always recognized, however, for
there must have been variation in this matter, depending
on ecological adaptation.

Because outmarriage was practiced, and because the wife
joined the husband, there were certain structural consequences. Obviously, the local band contained married
women from one or more other bands and in turn lost its
own nubile females. Also obviously, children of these marriages grew up in their father's localities and had only sporadic and more socially distant contacts with their mother's
bands, even though mother's group and father's group were
of equal genealogical nearness to a child. The result was
that the local band's members (except for the wives) became
patrilineally related (from our point of view). Because of
this, anthropologists have often called this kind of group
a *patrilineal band*. This term is unfortunate in one respect:
it carries the connotation that the group conceptualizes the
patrilineal descent line, and further, that membership in
the group is essentially a matter of reckoning descent.

Sometimes an even more unwarranted assumption is
made: that the mode of virilocal marital residence was followed in conformity with the rule of descent, as a sort of
consequence of it. This requires the belief that the more
abstract and far-fetched descent reckoning was first in time
and that groups were formed secondarily. Scientifically, it
is better to make fewer assumptions. The social structure
can be accounted for easily enough, and once the exchange
of women between groups became consistent, or modal, as
in virilocal residence, then the structure became consistent.
From the point of view of membership through generations
it is better to call such a band *patrilocal*—meaning by this
that children grow up in the band of the father, not the
mother—for there are no half-hidden assumptions concerning descent reckoning and descent lines in that term. Patrilineal descent, as a significant conception related to the

formation of groups, can be shown to be a much later development in the evolution of social organization and to
have certain social consequences not found in band society.

Given a local residential basis for the band, and given
local (or band) reciprocal exogamy and virilocality as social
modes rather than mere individual expediencies, the most
probable kind of early human social organization is created. The important groups in the social structure are: (1)
nuclear families, (2) extended families made up of the part-
time association of adult brothers and their nuclear families
(the degree of their actual residential association in a camp
could vary greatly from infrequent to usual), and (3) the
total patrilocal band. Because a band is exogamous and
named and has some coherence as an occasional action unit
above the level of extended families it is something more
than a *mere* residential unit: certain conceptual factors have
been added. This local unit is not the whole society, however, because exogamy creates ties of a certain kind—affinal
ties—with one or more other such units.

From the point of view of any individual the kinship
world consists, in its broadest conception, of two kinds of
people. There are the people of one's own band and there
are those others with whom affinal relationships obtain, the
"in-laws." This dichotomy can be thought of in various ways:
there are "father's people" and "mother's people"; there are
"own people" (the intimate ones) and "other people"; later
in life, there are "my people" and "wife's people," and
"son-in-law's" or "daughter-in-law's people." This kind of
division is of considerable social importance in all societies,
but in the small social world of early man it must have been
of enormous significance. When the two groups are named,
as they often are, anthropologists call it a *moiety* organization. There is some ambiguity, however, for sometimes this
word has been used to characterize *any* dual division,
whether it has merely ceremonial or recreational functions
or is truly affinal. From here on, the word moiety will apply

only to the exogamic divisions, and I shall use it whether or not they are given objective, distinguishing names.[6]

STATUSES

So far the fundamental groups of the social structure and most important rules related to them have been named. Now we turn to the ways in which the different kinds of *social persons* created by the rules and the resultant structure are designated in terms of statuses and assigned appropriate attributes for the regulation of their interpersonal conduct.

Kinship Terminology

Egocentric statuses have as their point of reference an individual, an *Ego*. Whereas every Ego holds in his head the full complement of terms, the persons who occupy the status positions differ from one Ego to another—my "father" might be your "brother."

Familistic statuses are those that differentiate social positions by criteria found within familistic societies such as bands. Generation and age, sex, marital state, household dyadic positions, and affinal relationship are the most usual criteria for this kind of internal differentiation.

Status terms are classificatory devices; that is, a term refers to a category and is not identical with an individual person. Even though only one person might occupy the position at a time, another can occupy it later. As a category it is defined in terms of certain attributes which the person occupying it will hold, or should hold, but the cate-

---

[6] The moiety categories can be significant without having sociocentric names attached, for the egocentric kinship terminology can also reveal the fundamental difference. See the following discussion of status terminology.

gory is not defined in terms of *all* of the attributes of the person.

Here is one reason for denying the argument made by Malinowski (1930) and accepted so definitively by Murdock (1949), that the classificatory kinship system began in the nuclear family and was extended outward. In an individual nuclear family the status "father" would be identical with the particular person, John, and "mother" with Mabel. How would, or could, John and Mabel become members of a *class* or *category* as persons, unless it were desirable to associate them with a *kind* of person, similar in certain ways, and separate them from still other kinds? Let us, instead, proceed from the other end, with the assumption that individuals have no trouble knowing all of the necessary attributes of the unique persons in their nuclear family, but that greater social difficulties lie in the secondary, more distant relationships, and with a related assumption that etiquette —order in interpersonal behavior as defined by society—is the more required in relations among families than within them. The broadest distinction in the kinship world is that of the moiety, of "own" and "other" persons. And here, too, lie some of the greatest universal differences in etiquette; one need only be reminded of the differences between "father" and "father-in-law," "mother" and "mother-in-law," "brother" and "brother-in-law."

There is another familistic criterion of status which seems at least as significant as the moiety distinction. This is generational standing. The relation of parents to children has, of course, universal recognition. Parents love their children, nurture them, rule them, and educate them. But why should generational standing be made a status? Why can't John and Mabel love and rule John, Jr. as *John* and *Mabel* ruling *Jackie*, rather than as the *older generation* ruling the *younger generation*? The answer is that they can and do. But they have to teach Jackie about parents and children, respect for the older generation, and so on, in general and categorical terms so that he will know how to act with persons who are *not* John and Mabel.

There is another important social distinction which may be the oldest and most fundamental of all, as well as the one related to the greatest number of joys, problems, and dangers. This is the universally observed distinction between males and females. However, since it is universally found as a status criterion at all stages of cultural evolution, sex distinction does not figure in the theoretical problems of social organization which arise from changes and differences in kind of patterning. Hence we may in this discussion, after acknowledging its importance and generality, ignore it.

Now we have a simple model of a social structure cross-cut by two different criteria of status (not including sex distinctions): the own-other affinal distinction and the distinction between the two adjacent generations. All the members of society except grandparents or grandchildren are now classed as one of four kinds of social persons. Any person is to Ego: (1) own generation, own group; (2) own generation, other group; (3) adjacent generation, own group; (4) adjacent generation, other group. (I have used "adjacent generation" because I have not specified whether Ego is in this case an elder or a youngster. I have skipped grandparents-grandchild terms because they are usually the same word, "self-reciprocal"; that is, because of the socially nonfunctional nature of such a relationship a distinction is not always made between these two generations.) [7]

It may be useful to elaborate this model in terms of genealogical reckoning, if only to show how complicated it can seem when our own society's conceptions are introduced. In Category 1 are Ego's own siblings and his father's brothers' children and usually his mother's sisters' children (who could

---

[7] A fuller discussion of this seemingly peculiar phenomenon will be given in Chapter 3.

be the same persons if the common primitive custom of a
brother-sister exchange was followed). Both of these groups
of children are called *parallel cousins* in anthropological
parlance. In Category 2 are *cross-cousins* (mother's brothers'
and perhaps father's sisters' children), who are also potentially brothers- and sisters-in-law, and spouse. In Category
3, if Ego is in the elder generation, are own children and
brothers' children (parallel nephews and nieces) and perhaps
wife's sisters' children (also parallel nephews and nieces),
and, if the band is fairly large, Ego's male parallel cousins'
children ("cousins once removed").[8] If Ego is a youngster,
Category 3 contains own father, mother, father's brother,
perhaps father's male parallel cousins, and (if brother-sister
marriage exchange) mother's sister or female parallel cousin.
Category 4 contains (if Ego is an elder) daughter-in-law, sister's children, wife's brother's (Ego's brother-in-law's) children (cross-nephews and nieces). If Ego is a youngster, Category 4 contains father-in-law and mother-in-law (who are
also mother's brother and, before she married, father's sister) and male parallel cousins of mother's brother (for Ego,
cross-cousins once removed—in generation). One sees above
how such a simple four-part system based on the two obviously important criteria of generation and intermarriage
can seem to present difficulties if we try to analyze and explain it in terms of our own notions of kinship.

This simple kinship system is probably the most widespread type in the primitive world. It is essentially the so-
called *bifurcate-merging* found scattered over the world
among most hunting-gathering bands and many tribes. According to the perspective taken here, the fact that the bifurcate-merging kinship system is widespread in the modern
primitive world, hundreds of thousands of years after the

---

[8] To anticipate a possible objection: there is often a variation in the
status terms given Ego's male cross-cousin's children and Ego's sister's
children among virilocal bands known ethnologically in modern times.
This will be discussed in Chapter 3.

Ego's Parents' Generation

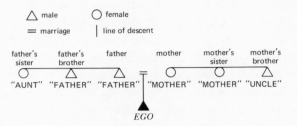

Cousins of *ego,* children of the relatives designated in the diagram above, are similarly divided into two types, one of which is merged with *ego's* lineal group, following the pattern set above. In anthropological terminology, those in *ego's* lineal group are called *parallel cousins,* while those distinguished from them (mother's brother's and father's sister's children) are called *cross cousins.*

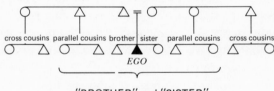

"BROTHER" and "SISTER"

Relatives in *ego's* children's generation are also separated into the parallel category and the cross category. The diagram below shows the parallels in *ego's* local group. It is obvious that a difference in social propinquity is correlated with the separation of parallel relatives from cross relatives.

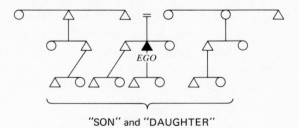

"SON" and "DAUGHTER"

SOURCE: Elman R. Service, *Profiles in Ethnology,* 2nd ed. (New York: Harper & Row, 1963), p. 13.

origin of human society, is no reason for assuming it was not also the earliest full-fledged one. Consistent unilocal marital residence modes and reciprocal group exogamy (which imply each other) are all that are required as *developments* to go along with a universally human social feature, the importance of adjacent generations as a status consideration. The persistence of such a system should not be surprising. It works. And one reason why it works so well could be that it is so simple.

But this reasoning should not be regarded as an argument for the universality or inevitability of the bifurcate-merging system. There are many other simple systems which diverge through adaptation to special environmental circumstances. For example, the central Australian environment results in a rather special embellishment, and the modern Eskimo's environment in a special simplification. The consequences of these peculiar adaptations are amenable to the same kind of analysis as the bifurcate-merging system, however, and they will be discussed in Chapter 3.

3

The Social Organization
of Bands

⫷⫸ The paleolithic era—the span of time from the origins of culture until the beginning of the domestication of plants and animals—was a time when there were no forms of economy higher than hunting-gathering bands.[1] Once the neolithic era began and the tribes gradually expanded, some bands were transformed, others possibly obliterated, and the remainder pushed into, or confined to, ecological areas where domestication of plants and animals was not feasible. Still higher stages of cultural development, culminating in industrial civilizations, came to dominate these earlier levels of culture until remnants of the original kind of hunting-gathering bands which once covered the face of the earth

---

[1] At one time paleolithic and neolithic referred only to types of stones tools, but more recently neolithic has come to refer to cultures based on agriculture and/or animal husbandry. Paleolithic, correlatively, could be understood now as referring to hunting-gathering, pre-neolithic society. Since it seems evident that chipped stone tools were used by prehuman primates and may long antedate human society or culture (cf. Washburn, 1960) there is a further reason for not allowing this otherwise well-established concept to be restricted to a kind of stone-tool manufacture.

are found in modern times only in marginal, out-of-the-way places.

All societies at the band level of integration are foragers of wild food. Not all wild-food foragers are at the band level, however. Along the northwest coast of North America were large populations of maritime peoples whose environment was so remarkably bountiful that they lived in complex communities at the level of chiefdoms. In California were other societies who lived in such natural abundance that their societies also transcended the band level. The paleolithic era thus may well have had some such forms of society in addition to bands. However that may be, the band level of integration is by far the most frequent among known hunters and gatherers and must have been the characteristic, though perhaps not universal, form of social organization during the paleolithic era.

TYPES OF BANDS

Julian Steward codified the ethnologically known bands into two polar types, which he called the *patrilineal* band and the *composite* band (1955, Chs. 7, 8). The patrilineal band is a group which is exogamous and virilocal. The composite band is one which lacks exogamic rules and explicit marital residence customs. It is, so to speak, more of an expedient agglomeration than a structured society.

It was earlier explained why patrilineal is felt to be misleading, hence that kind of band will now be called "patrilocal" inasmuch as the most significant consequence of virilocality for the composition of the band is that children grow up among the father's relatives. Composite has its difficulties, too, as a term for the other kind of band, but it is fairly well established and a more appropriate alternative does not come to mind.

These are the extremes of types of bands. Many modern societies are intermediate to these in certain respects. There are no purely uxorilocal-matrilocal band societies.[2]

The bands known to us in modern times which have been important in anthropological thought, particularly with respect to ideas about "origins of society," "early man," and Steward's conception of "cultural ecology" (1955, Chs. 7, 8), are listed below, following Steward, but somewhat rearranged and with a few additions. They range in type of social organization from clear-cut patrilocal bands at one extreme to composite bands at the other. This ordering also seems to conform to relatively isolated aboriginal conditions at the time of description on one extreme to breakdown and readaptation under the influence of civilization at the other. This ordering does not, however, appear to correlate clearly with differences in the kind, variety, or variability of food available, nor any other particular characteristic of the natural habitat alone, but rather, with aspects of the superorganic environment.

Patrilocal Bands

AUSTRALIANS. The Australian bands, described prior to their depopulation due to introduced diseases and before they were dispossessed from their native territories, all had a patrilocal band organization along with a number of sodality-like embellishments. It would seem that the whole

---

[2] Sometimes matrilineality has been attributed to certain Australian groups, but this seems to be a semantic confusion. To be sure there are "matrilineal social clans," as among the Dieri. These are not bands, however, but nonlocal kin sodalities with affiliation (not descent) through the mother. Band membership, however, is through the father, that is, the bands are patrilocal (see Elkin, 1931). Radcliffe-Brown (1956) has also described the confusion of concepts with reality that has resulted in "matrilines" from the anthropologists' notebooks of genealogy being ascribed to the actual social structure in Australia. He reaffirms convincingly the continent-wide *aboriginal* existence of patrilocal local groups, as has Birdsell more recently (1970).

continent contained bands of this type (Elkin, 1954, pp. 44–48, 80; Radcliffe-Brown, 1956; Birdsell, 1970). The natural environment of Australia varies enormously, from the rainy coastal regions with their abundance of food that permitted a relatively dense and sedentary aboriginal population to the extremely arid central regions with a very thin population of scattered wanderers. Despite the great demographic differences, however, the patrilocal social structure was characteristic throughout. And in terms of sheer numbers, the Australian societies add greatly to the count of patrilocal examples—if one is impressed by statistics in problems of this sort.

TASMANIANS. The natives of Tasmania were similar in most important respects to the Australians.

THE ONA. The inland Indians of Tierra del Fuego were patrilocal and strictly observed band territoriality. Subsistence was based largely on the hunting of guanaco.

THE TEHUELCHE. Before the introduction of the horse the Indians of Patagonia were organized similarly to the Ona and with a similar subsistence base.

SOUTHERN CALIFORNIANS. The Shoshonean Serrano, Cahuilla, Luiseño, and the Yuman Diegueño had patrilocal bands. Subsistence was based on acorns and wild seeds and population was fairly dense in the area, although the bands themselves remained small (about fifty people per band according to Steward [1955, p. 133]).

INDIANS OF THE CENTRAL DESERT OF BAJA CALIFORNIA. These Indians are extinct but have been recently described from historical archives by Aschmann (1959) and Massey (1961). The environment was extremely arid, with subsistence resources scattered and variable and population thin. The social organization was of patrilineal (patrilocal) bands in definite territories, averaging about 75 persons each (Massey, 1961, p. 415). Aschmann's account is particularly useful for its detailed exposition of the social effects of later depopulation due to foreign diseases.

PHILIPPINE NEGRITOS. Steward (1955, pp. 130–131) believes that these bands were originally patrilineal but that they became composite during the past century. They exploited a mountainous tropical forest of varied resources.

THE SEMANG OF THE MALAY PENINSULA. Steward lists the Semang as patrilineal, noting band exogamy and virilocal residence. As in the case of the Philippine Negritos, however, the evidence is not very clear, and because they were enclaved among stronger neighbors there is the additional complication of possible acculturation.

CENTRAL AFRICAN NEGRITOS. The pygmies of the Ituri forest were predominantly hunters of big game with some economic symbiosis with Negro farmers. It could be argued that the patrilocal band organization was borrowed from the Negroes, or imposed by them. Steward (1955, p. 128) does not think so, but because of the possibility we should probably not rely on this group as an example. For what it is worth, I agree with Steward, however, that such things as virilocal residence and band exogamy are unlikely to be diffused, borrowed, or otherwise products of "contact." (It might well be added that in his study Colin Turnbull [1961] disputes the view that these people were so importantly influenced by their Negro "overlords" as has been believed.)

THE BUSHMEN OF SOUTH AFRICA. Steward cites the Northwestern Bushmen, such as the Heikum, as patrilineal bands. The Bushmen probably are not good examples of either patrilocal or composite bands, however. Most of them have long been truly subject to Negro overlords. Those few who are still independent are clearly refugees with extremely variable group composition.

Composite Bands

THE NORTHERN ALGONKIANS. Many of the Indians of Eastern Canada have had patrilocal nuclear families since their involvement in the fur trade. Steward (1955, p. 145) believes that, "In aboriginal times, however, when hunting of large game, which ranges in herds far beyond the limits of the family trapping territories, was the principal subsistence activity, the multifamily, composite band was probably not only the political unit but also the landowning subsistence and social unit." It will be shown in subsequent pages that there is actually some evidence that the Algonkians were not composite aboriginally.

THE NORTHERN ATHABASKANS. These Indians of Northwestern Canada had large and composite bands aboriginally, according to Steward (1955, pp. 146–148), for the same reason as the Algonkians. They were hunters of large herds of migratory game, hence the bands were very large, expedient, and often of unrelated families, making band exogamy unnecessary. As in the case of the Algonkians, an argument will be presented later that casts doubt on this proposition.

THE ANDAMAN ISLANDERS. The Andamanese had bands which observed territorial boundaries and some local exogamy, but there was no consistent virilocality. Thus they make a negative case for Steward's argument, for the forest products were plentiful and varied and there was no dependence on large herds of migratory game. Steward (1955, p. 149) admits this, but feels that these bands were composite because the frequent adoption of children confused band membership and made marriages possible within the band. Later in this chapter a different explanation will be offered.

THE YAHGAN OF TIERRA DEL FUEGO. Steward did not include the Yahgan in his discussion of either patrilineal or composite bands. As described ethnologically, however, they are an example of composite bands similar to the Andamanese, that is with band territoriality but no consistent marriage practices with respect to it. This could not have been predicted from their subsistence base, however, for they are gatherers and fishermen, with primary dependence on mussels and other coastal products. There was no expedient mixing of unrelated, hence marriageable, families in the

pursuit of migratory game or any other such variable resources and the bands "occupied more or less fixed separate
localities" (Cooper, 1946, p. 84). The Yahgan are, then, like
the Andamanese, clearly a negative case for Steward's theory,
and their organization—rather, the lack of it—must be explained in some other terms.

Anomalous Bands

THE WESTERN SHOSHONE OF NEVADA. Steward did not include
these Indians in his discussion of patrilineal and composite
bands because he felt that the exigencies of their adaptation
to the natural environment had so fragmented them that
they were not bands at all but were only at what he called
"the family level of integration." He has discussed them at
length (1938 and 1955), however, in terms of his environmental theory. We want to consider them in the present
chapter because an argument can be made that they might
well have had bands aboriginally, and that the later fragmentation can be explained by their superorganic environment.
THE ESKIMO. The Eskimo also were considered by Steward
to be family level and thus were not listed as bands. But,
like the Shoshone, they will be reconsidered here as possibly
having been bands aboriginally, with fragmentation a result
of modern influence.

It could be argued from mere inspection of the foregoing
lists that the patrilocal band is more to be expected among
hunting-gathering bands than is either the composite or
the anomalous family-level type. Patrilocal bands are not
only more numerous, but also seem to exist under extremely
varying conditions of natural environment and within all
the variations in subsistence base implied in such a scatter.
It can also be argued on the basis of theoretical functional necessity that the patrilocal band is the likely form

of organization at such low population densities under aboriginal conditions. For this reason the judgment was made that this was probably the earliest full form of social organization as well as the most adaptable to varying conditions. If this judgment is provisionally accepted, however, then a major problem concerning the nature of the adaptation of band society must be discussed and resolved. The problem has two aspects. (1) If characteristics of the natural environment are related to demography, but if a social organizational type such as the patrilocal band can occur under varied conditions of natural environment and related demography, then what *is* the relation of the social organization of bands to demography and habitat?

(2) If the patrilocal type is taken as expectable among hunting-gathering bands, then what about the composite bands of the Canadian Algonkians and Athabaskans, the Andamanese, and the Yahgan? And what about the anomalous family-level Eskimo and Western Shoshone? If for the reasons given above and in the previous chapter, we are to take the more numerous patrilocal bands as the normal type, then the deviant composite and anomalous types have to be explained. And again, we want to know what adaptation to habitat has to do with the explanation.

The remainder of this chapter is organized so as to answer these questions. First, the patrilocal band generally as a type of social organization and in relation to demography and environment will be discussed. As has been already implied, two conceptual devices will be used to attempt a solution to the problem: the concept *sodality* in relation to demographic residential groups, and the conception of adaptation to *total environment,* which includes the superorganic (cultural) aspect as well as organic and inorganic aspects.

Second, the composite and anomalous bands will be discussed in the light of relevant ethnohistorical data. Again, the nature of adaptation to a new superorganic environment—in these cases that created by influences of the invading civilization—is the main conceptual ingredient in the attempted explanations.

THE PATRILOCAL BAND

Much of the discussion which follows considers the patrilocal band from an ideal-typical standpoint, only occasionally referring to some particular variation rather than trying to summarize the various kinds listed. This is necessary in order to stay on the general level with respect to certain broad theoretical points. A departure from the ideal-typical, highly generalized, discussion is made when the problem of the adaptation of bands is considered, however, for at that point particular geographical and demographic variation is relevant to the argument.

Rules

The most significant rules among patrilocal bands are *reciprocal band exogamy* and the associated *virilocal marital residence* mode, for it is these that create the patrilocal structure of the band. Unilocal residence, of course, presupposes local exogamy, but the question of residence is crucial, for it can in theory be variable with exogamy constant.

It is apparent from mere inspection of the list of patrilocal bands with their great variety of natural environmental conditions that virilocal residence modes are not caused by any particular kind of habitat or source of food. The argument was made in the previous chapter that virilocality is expectable in exogamous band society because of the importance of the solidarity of the males in hunting, sharing game, and particularly in offense-defense. This necessity could be expected to continue from early to late times, until the epoch of modern acculturation when hunting diminished in importance, or individualized fur-trapping took its place, and especially when the aborigines became enclaved within a powerful modern society which enforced peace. Particular instances will be discussed later in this chapter.

Certain other rules are widely prevalent, though not universal, in band society. Perhaps most striking are those marriages called *levirate* and *sororate*. Both of these preserve the delayed reciprocal aspect of a marriage pact between familistic groupings. The pact is maintained in the case of the death of a husband by having the brother of the deceased take his place. Thus the woman and her children remain as part of the group into which she was given. This is the levirate. The obverse is the sororate, which is less frequent but quite common. In this case if the wife dies she is replaced by her sister, usually the younger. Again, reciprocity is preserved.

Another very common rule attributed to patrilocal bands is *cross-cousin marriage*. It is perhaps doubtful that this form of marriage should be considered truly a rule, however, for it is in large measure a construct of anthropologists rather than something conceptualized by the members of the society. Given an exogamous band in stable circumstances, then there are no marriageable partners among relatives of one's own generation except cross-cousins of several degrees—that is, relatives of *own* generation in *other* band or moiety. This is, so to speak, a resultant of reciprocal group exogamy. In our own genealogical system those persons would be not only cross-cousins of the first degree, for depending on the size of the other group or groups of affinal relatives there might be more distant cross-cousins, such as daughters of mother's male parallel cousins as well as of her own brothers.

Sometimes territorial groups are of such a restricted size that only certain cross-cousins are found in mother's original band, whereas those of more distant degree are found in still another neighboring group, though of the same moiety.

In some parts of Australia the bands are of just such a size and the rules of marriage proscribe marriage (of a man) with someone of mother's own band as too close; marriage is prescribed with a girl of a more distant band. Such groups would include cross-cousins of further degree, hence anthropologists call it a "rule of second cross-cousin marriage." We are probably imputing more precision to this than is warranted, however, for the Australians themselves may well see the situation not in terms of genealogy but in terms of locality and groups instead: Ego marries a girl of such-and-such a local group in a certain generation and not into his mother's own group.

Another kind of cross-cousin marriage is what has been called "prescriptive matrilateral cross-cousin marriage," meaning that Ego marries the cross-cousin standing in the classificatory relationship of mother's brother's daughter to him but cannot marry father's sister's daughter. This asymmetry causes the group reciprocity to be indirect between particular bands, so that, for example, group A gives wives to B, B to C, C to D, and D back to A. As Leach (1951) has shown, however, the groups are themselves arranged as two sides, so that the exchange is in their minds directly reciprocal between two moieties. This kind of marriage rule is uncommon at the band level and has been well-described for only one such society, the Murngin of Australia (Warner, 1964).

Social Structure

Both the internal structure of each band and the external associations among certain bands are created by rules of exogamy and virilocal residence. A *natural* biological group is amorphous except for the dominance hierarchy, sexual pairs, if any, and mother-child dyads. However, once reciprocal virilocal marriage exchanges between two such groups have become modal for more than one generation then the relations between the two groups have a character invested with new, cultural, determinants. The simplest is the common moiety arrangement of two, or often several, groups arranged as two sides which intermarry. The moiety may be named and rigidified, as it so frequently is among the Australian bands, or it may be unnamed and revealed only in the egocentric status terminology, but the strictness of conduct required between people of in-law status, or own and other (as it is frequently conceptualized), are always of great significance in family life.

The marriage rule which creates these groups, separated in certain ways, united in others, simultaneously creates a new kind of internal structure in each local group. Now all the people are each a part of their *father's* group, not the mother's; she remains in some sense an outsider, particularly in the early years of the marriage. Within each generation, every person is in close association with his siblings (until the sisters have married out) and parallel cousins (children of the group's males of the ascendant, or father's, generation).

The nuclear family, as noted in the previous chapter, is a creation of the marriage rule and of the sexual division of labor which results in the husband of the conjugal dyad becoming the protector and provider of the wife, and ultimately of her offspring. Hence husband-father, wife-mother, offspring, and perhaps an aged dependent make up the most cohesive unit in band society. There is no significant division of labor or specialization above the level of the conjugal dyad and therefore, depending on circumstances, nuclear families may forage more or less alone within the band's range.

The patrilocal band varies in size within certain limits. If it is too small to be viable it ceases to exist, of course, and then we do not know about it. If it is large enough, and particularly when the food supply is of the kind that permits relatively permanent villages, then it can be a marriage isolate, including exogamous groups within itself, and has thus ascended to a higher level of integration. According to Steward's population figures on the various examples of the patrilocal band (1955, pp. 135, 140), they vary in size from thirty persons, at least, to over one hundred. Population density is one person or less—often much less—per square mile.

Recent research has shown Steward's figures to be basically sound. Working groups of six to eight males form a normal unit, a number that fits a twenty-five-member band. Archaeological studies of "living-floors" suggest a similar size for prehistoric bands (Pfeiffer 1969, pp. 332–333). The dialectical *tribe*—that is, collections of bands that share language and culture to the extent that they have a felt unity as against others—seems to cluster around 500, but this is not otherwise a corporate group—a true tribe.

The demographic distribution of the members of a band at any given time depends on the food being gathered or hunted at a particular season or year. In desert areas such as much of Australia, Nevada, or Baja California, individual nuclear families spend much of the time foraging alone, or at best sometimes forming a camp of only a few nuclear families headed by brothers. However, it is common for the families of brothers to remain more contiguous to each other than to others even when dispersed; hence there is a relatively discernible residential group within the band. This is the "patrilaterally extended family" in anthropological parlance. Presumably less frequently, the whole band may camp together in seasons of good foraging to hold ceremonies or other diversions. In other areas which are richer, but in which dependence is primarily on gathered food or shellfish, the nuclear families also spend considerable time alone. Where big-game hunting is very important, as in the Central African forests, all members of the band camp together more of the time, inasmuch as the hunting of such game often requires the cooperation of a fairly large number of people and the bag of such game will ordinarily feed them all simultaneously.

The amount of dispersion or aggregation of band members also depends on whether or not peace is prevalent. It is apparent that this factor has varied greatly in historic epochs, with fighting often greatly increased when the first contacts with Europeans produced dislocations and migrations, and greatly diminished in later times when control had been established.

To these variables should be added the probability that still other different kinds of sporadic activities will involve larger groups than the corporate local group. Befu and Plotnicov (1962) have shown that among corporate descent groups (in tribal society) the minimal group, the family-household, is most consistently engaged in corporate economic activities. The local group (normally a lineage) will add corporate political functions; and the largest dispersed group is more likely to feature corporate religious, especially ceremonial, activities. There seems to be no reason for doubting that a similar division of cultural labor would apply to the various levels of agglomeration in a society of bands.

All of the above remarks are made in order to emphasize that for a band to be a band the people do not have to be closely, physically associated as a face-to-face residential group at all times, or even much of the time. Some of our best examples of patrilocal bands are from the central desert of Australia, where meetings of relatives would seem to be the most infrequent of any bands; on the other hand, the members of the composite bands of some Canadian Athabaskans are in much more frequent association in modern times. This is by way of emphasizing that the influence of habitat on the structure of bands is significant in establishing limits to the size of the agglomerated band, but need not directly influence the internal structure.

Bands are frequently defined in terms of the territory that

they conventionally inhabit. Often the name of the band is the name of the territory. This should not be taken to mean that these territories are necessarily closed, with boundaries rigorously defined against *all* outsiders, however. One of the important functions of exogamy is that of opening territories so that peaceful movements can take place among them, and particularly so that any large temporary variations in food resources can be taken advantage of by the related groups. Territoriality seems to be often largely a social matter; it is a way of describing membership in a group rather than being rigorously a matter of economic exploitation. Among known patrilocal bands there are great variations in the observance of territorial boundaries. The Ona of Tierra del Fuego and certain Australians are perhaps the best examples of strictness in this, whereas the other Fuegians and the Northern Australians do not observe boundaries particularly, although they have a strong feeling for their band "country" in a general sense, and the band membership is described in terms of locality.

At this point it is appropriate to confront directly the question of geographical determination of social organization. Band society is closer to nature and controls it less than do higher levels of culture, and may therefore be assumed to be more directly influenced by the nature of the food supply available. Yet it seems apparent that there are peoples with a similar patrilocal band structure who nevertheless occupy extremely variable kinds of habitats, who range from hunters of big game to dependence on gathered food and occupy localities that are territorially "closed" (that is, boundaries observed and defended) in some instances and open in others. That amount of food, kind of food, and its seasonal and yearly variation, affect the *demographic* character of band society is unquestionable. As noted, some bands are dispersed into single nuclear families over enormous areas most of the time, some are dispersed in some seasons and agglomerated in others, and some are fairly consistently agglomerated most of the time. But bands of patrilocal social structure are found in any of these circumstances. Among the unstructured composite and anomalous bands there is a similar lack of congruity between habitat and demography on the one hand, and social structure, or its relative absence, on the other.

The theory of geographical determination of social organization, on the band level at least, has become widely accepted in anthropology and no one seems to have questioned it. It was first proposed in its modern formulation by Steward in 1936 and restated in 1955.[3] In his version it is not simply a matter of subsistence resources, however, for Steward allows for the effects of certain other factors. Some of these have been mentioned in the earlier passages which discuss his listing of bands. Steward's theory has been accepted by others (for example, Forde, 1947, pp. 218–219; Sahlins, 1959, p. 190), however, in terms of subsistence resources alone. C. D. Forde (1947), for example, in speaking of rudimentary bands, says:

> The food supply in any locality, whether it be a harvest of pinyon nuts or wild grass seeds among the Paiute, or the seal population at winter and spring hunting grounds, and the caribou herd migrating through an inland valley among the Central Eskimo, is so unpredictable or so widely scattered that the tendency for particular kinsfolk in any generation to form coherent exclusive groups is frustrated by the opportunism enforced on the individual and the household by the ecological situation. Systematic organisation through rules governing the residence of families, the affiliation of individuals to groups and succession to status or economic rights in accordance with descent, is lacking because the ties latent in parentage and siblinghood are prevented from formalized expression in the social organisation [pp. 218–219].

---

[3] Steward used the word *ecology,* not geography. I have changed this because the word ecology has become used so hysterically these days, creating images of poisons and dumptrucks, that all clarity is lost.

It will be shown in later pages that the band societies in their *aboriginal* form do not in fact correspond to the social organizations they are supposed to have by the above explanation. Such societies as the Central Australians, for example, would seem to have the most variable food supplies, both seasonally and annually, of any bands known, yet their social organization is noteworthy for its variety of clean-cut groups, sodalities, statuses, virilocal residence modes, local exogamy, territoriality, and so on. The geographical argument, it is apparent, is useful when demography alone is under discussion, but there is more to social organization than demography. *Human* social organization is cultural and a form of explanation which is adequate for societies of wild animals is not sufficient for human societies, even those at the lowest levels of complexity.

Social structure includes not only residential groups but also sodalities. Social organization, a still broader concept, includes not only social structure but also the status network and ideological rules. Residential groups are the parts of the social organization which are most directly demographic and which are the most affected by geographical situations—though not these alone. Sodalities, on the other hand, come about precisely when the residential factor in sociality is weak or does not do all that is required in social life. Thus those very Central Australians who have such a formalized and explicit social organization in all aspects are those whose demographic arrangement of residential groups is the most variable by season and year, whose membership is ordinarily the most scattered, and whose association is the most fortuitous, who should be the most "frustrated . . . by the ecological situation," and whose "ties latent in parenthood and siblinghood are prevented from formalized expression in the social organization."

That those desert-dwellers of Australia are not "frustrated" must be due to their having formed sodalities to do the social job that the weak and impermanent residential groups could not do. And in fact this much is so: the Central Australians have more kinds of sodalities than any people at the band level unless some of the Ge-speaking Indians of Brazil are to be included in the band category. There are male age-graded or generation sodalities dramatized by the great initiation ceremonies; there are the famed totemic "clans," some through maternal succession to membership and others paternal; and there are blood-brotherhoods of a sort. More striking are the churinga-storehouses and elaborate mythology and ceremony connected with them that make locality a clearer and more meaningful social conception than it would be without such sodality-like embellishments. A further interesting characteristic of Australia is that a regular progression from the rich, rainy, coastal areas with their large and relatively sedentary local groups to the desert interior with its widely scattered, small, wandering population is equally a progression from *least* formality and complication in the former to *greatest* in the latter area (Yengoyan, 1968).

Sodalities seem to come about in some relation to their need. Central Australians needed them more than did coastal Australians, whose residential bands were large and much more closely agglomerated. Thus geography-demography does not prevent or frustrate sodalities, nor any status complication associated with them. If anything, the opposite is to be expected in that when seasonal and yearly fluctuations in food resources prevent the formation of cohesive residential groups, it is more likely that the social organization itself will become more complex-seeming and more formal as sodalities and associated statuses come about to make possible cooperation in military, economic, and ceremonial affairs.

To summarize briefly, and to emphasize perhaps immoderately: it has been argued so far that rules of reciprocal band exogamy are related to peacemaking alliance and offense-defense situations, that is, to the superorganic environment rather than to food-getting alone. The rule of virilocal residence is also related to male cooperation in offense-defense, and not always to hunting alone. Why would such peoples as the Southern California acorn- and seed-gatherers have virilocal residence if hunting cooperation or the hunters' familiarity with their own territory were the only relevant factors?

Band exogamy and virilocal residence make a patrilocal band. When subsistence factors cause band members to be widely scattered so that the residential factor is weak then the band comes to be more like a sodality, with insignia, mythology, ceremony, emphasis on kinship statuses, and so on, which make the band a more coherent and cohesive unity.[4]

Sodality, then, is a culturally created factor in social structure which can intrude itself between geography-demography and the rest of the organization. No bands are *simply* residential agglomerations; all have some sodality-like characteristics in their sociality. But the number of those features and their relative strength is likely to be in inverse ratio to the strength of the residential factor. When the residential factor and sodality factors are both weak then

---

[4] In one illuminating instance Steward shows how such sodality-like practices can function. The Shoshoneans of Southern California had "patrilineal" bands in spite of a demographic, or residential, situation which would seem to preclude their existence. Steward says of them (1955):

Death observances were matters of private ritual among most of these bands, but the Shoshoneans of Southern California developed them into a ceremony which greatly strengthened group cohesion. An annual mourning ceremony was held under the direction of a special ceremonial leader, while images of the deceased were burned and myths were recited to commemorate the dying god. This ceremony seems to have contributed greatly to the cohesion of Shoshonean bands, and it may partly explain why the bands continued to regard themselves as kin groups and to practice exogamy after they became dislocated from their territories, scattered, and lost genealogical knowledge of their relationship to each other [pp. 141–142].

of course the society is more reduced to the family-level attributed to the Western Shoshone and some Eskimo. But this is rare and due to special circumstances that will be discussed later.

Statuses

Inasmuch as band society is small, the greater proportion of statuses are familistic and egocentric. Relative age or generation, and sex distinctions, combined with the own-other dualism are the most gross and basic and provide the characteristics of the kinship (egocentric-familistic) status terminology. It is merely the distinction between generations, bifurcated by the affinal division of exogamous duality which makes the anthropologists' cross and parallel categories. This is essentially the so-called bifurcate-merging system.

Lowie (1928) first proposed the name bifurcate-merging for this widespread pattern. He believed that exogamy was the cause of it. Murdock (1947) reviewed this theory along with four others and made a statistical test of correlation of them in a large sample of societies. The theories additional to Lowie's were: Rivers', who ascribed the bifurcate-merging terminology to the influence of moieties; Kroeber's, which was that unilineal descent was the cause; Sapir's, that it resulted from levirate and sororate marriages; and Radcliffe-Brown's notion that a universal principle, "the social equivalence of brothers," was the cause.

The result of Murdock's test was suggestive and interesting, but not entirely conclusive. The reason it could not be conclusive seems to be that the concepts used were not sharp enough.[5]

---

[5] A further reason why correlation was not complete possibly lay in the sample. A number of the societies listed have undergone changes which could disjoint the terminological pattern from the factors related to its origin (Dole, 1957, pp. 173–177).

Two of the proposed causes are too general to yield a direct correlation with a specific terminological pattern, and the other three are too restrictive. Radcliffe-Brown's universal principle should, of course, match a universal terminological pattern; furthermore, like a great many "principles," it is merely a tautology and hence logically to be dismissed from further consideration. Exogamy is so general as a conception and has been given so many meanings in the literature that trouble was bound to result. It is apparent, however, that had Lowie meant group or local exogamy, which narrows the concept considerably, he would have come closer to the conception accepted in the present book.

Rivers' concept moiety could not yield a high correlation because it is at once too restrictive in one of its meanings and too general in another. Sometimes moiety means only *named* affinal dual divisions; but, as discussed earlier, the dual division often exists without being named sociocentrically, hence correlation on that basis would be lowered because in the ethnographic literature it is usual for only the named ones to be called moieties. On the other hand, it is also common in the literature for *any* named divisions to be called moieties, whether they have anything to do with exogamy and affines or not (there are named divisions that are ceremonial only and others that have to do only with competitive games).

Levirate-sororate marriages are clearly too restrictive; they *tend* to be stated as rules where reciprocal group exogamy prevails, but they need not be, and furthermore they could be easily overlooked by the ethnographer unless there were a number of deaths when he was present.

Kroeber's suggestion that unilineal kin groups cause bifurcate-merging is clearly off the mark, although it received the highest grade in Murdock's test. This must be because Kroeber, Murdock, and many others call *patrilocal* bands *patrilineal*, hence an enormous number of societies have unilinear kin groups in that sense, and they are all exogamous by definition. But this is no help, since a great number of societies with that kind of unilinear kin group do *not* have bifurcate-merging terminology. In other words, unilineality is conceived so broadly that it is nearly coterminous with exogamy and suffers the same deficiency as a correlation of, say, steel with automobiles or trees with apples.

"Reciprocal group exogamy," as a descriptive concept, seems to reduce the problem. Exogamy is too vague; all societies have exogamy in some sense. "Group" or "local" exogamy is better, but it need not necessarily result in the affinal dualism which, along with generational distinctions, is the obvious basic ingredient of the bifurcate-merging system. That is, a group might be exogamous but without any *consistent* relationship to any particular other groups: the affines of one family in a modern Eskimo village, for example, might be Indians; of another, Eskimos; and of another, European traders. Bifurcate-merging terminology is a *pattern* based on a society-wide affinal dualism; the implication is therefore of some stability and consistency. This is suggested well enough by the word "reciprocal" when applied to group relations. Moiety, if it were always used to mean an affinal dualism, whether named or not, seems useful and I have sometimes used it in that sense (although with fear of being misunderstood). Nevertheless, affinal dualism, moiety, or whatever you call it, is an obvious aspect of bifurcate-merging terminology; it is the behavioral and sometimes terminological side of a status arrangement of which bifurcate-merging terminology is the other (Tylor pointed this out long ago [1888, p. 262]). Let us say "aspect of" so not to be caught affirming one as prior to the other; to say that affinal dualism *causes* bifurcate-merging terminology—and the correlation should be perfect with a sample of undisturbed societies—would be to make a blatant tautology. It seems safer to go back a notch and suggest that reciprocal group marriage exchanges simultaneously cause both affinal dualism and bifurcate-merging terminology, if unilocal residence obtains so as to stabilize the duality in residential terms.[6]

It might be immediately objected that to say reciprocal group marriage exchange is the primary cause of bifurcate-merging terminology is to make the same error as in the case of exogamy as cause; that is, it is clearly associated not only with this terminology but also with some others, namely the Crow and Omaha patterns of terminology. This is so, but easily overcome as an objection. As we shall see in the next chapter, the Crow and Omaha patterns arise not in band society, but at the tribal level (and in a few cases still higher levels) and are merely a special embellishment for special reasons on what is still basically the bifurcate-merging pattern. Special circumstances yield special results; in these cases strong and large unilineal descent groups exert a new kind of influence on the terminological pattern. Exogamy, on the other hand, is much more broad than this; it is associated not only with bifurcate-merging and the related Crow and Omaha patterns but many others as well—with all others, one could argue.

There can arise, of course, variations and alternatives in particular features of the basic bifurcate-merging pattern even at the band level. The most usual ones occur under acculturative influence or degrees of breakdown of the patrilocal band structure, and therefore they will be reserved for later description.

Within the patrilocal category there seems to have occurred only one notable alteration in the otherwise widespread bifurcate-merging pattern. This is a terminology

---

[6] It should be understood that reciprocal exchanges are not necessarily between two and only two groups; any number can play so long as there are two sides. Also reciprocity need not be symmetrical, immediate, or direct, though some compensation or token is often given immediately for a wife when the exchange is indirect.

which Hocart (1928, pp. 180–182) has called the "cross-cousin pattern." At the band level it is found only among a few Australian groups. It is a modification of bifurcate-merging apparently caused by particular emphasis on the obligatory marriage of actual *first* cross-cousins rather than merely "own generation, other side," which includes first cross-cousins but does not single them out. This is not a pattern distinct from bifurcate-merging but rather an elaboration upon it.[7]

Other variations seem less significant, but might be given brief mention. Alternatives in grandparental terms are the most usual of these. In some band societies grandparent terms are the same as grandchild terms—"self-reciprocal"; sometimes they are not. The self-reciprocal type is widespread and needs explanation (Aberle, 1967).

It has been calculated that in very primitive societies the average life expectancy at birth is only twenty-two years and individuals who live as long as fifty years are rare (Dole, 1957, p. 26). Grandparents seldom live long enough to be personally known to their grandchildren, especially to adult grandchildren, hence this social relationship is usually nonfunctional. The self-reciprocal aspect can be thought of as a term for the kind of relationship itself rather than as designating categories of persons, that is, perhaps it merely means "separated by two generations." It could also be argued that even if grandparents do live long enough to have social relations with adult grandchildren there is little functional necessity for labeling them, that is, distinguishing them from each other with separate status terms. They are so far removed from each other in terms of actual, readily apparent, status and distinct authoritarian roles that there is little or no need to make the relationship more explicit with terminology. This view is consistent with our general assumption that status terms emphasize and make explicit *useful distinctions,* not extensions or "lumpings" in the social order.

---

[7] For a fuller discussion see Dole (1957, pp. 178–193).

Hocart (1931) pointed out that in many societies with such self-reciprocals a grandchild takes the same personal name as a grandparent, that is, is his namesake, as well as the same kinship term. We may take this as a further suggestive fact pointing to the relatively nonfunctional nature of this relationship; that is, there is no great social necessity for distinguishing grandchildren from grandparents with status terminology any more than by name. When grandparents *are* given separate terms, of course, the possibilities are various: if named moieties are a strong social consideration then there may be two kinds of grandparents by moiety membership and two by sex; if the moiety distinction is not so strong as a sociocentric status then mother's parents may be distinguished by Ego from father's.

Another variation depends on the relative emphasis given to sex. Affixes to the same term make the sexual distinction in some societies; in others the radical is different; sometimes the whole terminological pattern is changed, depending on whether the speaker, Ego, is a male or female.

The greatest variations in status terminology are not in the egocentric system, however, but in the sociocentric system. Sociocentric terms are more impersonal than egocentric terms in the sense that usually only one criterion of status is used in the social relationship, whereas in the egocentric bifurcate-merging terminology at least three (generation, sex, and affinal status) are used. Any social interaction based on nothing more than recognition of one criterion, such as generation, is highly impersonal. When more criteria of status enter the relationship it becomes more personal, the ultimate in this process occurring when finally the total social personality of the individual, with his completely idiosyncratic mixture of statuses, dominates the interaction. Then you are *you* instead of a member of a category. The gross, simple sociocentric terms thus are used in the social relations of people who are not closely or consistently associated with each other. Variations in the circumstances of different patrilocal bands would therefore affect the amount and significance of sociocentric terminology, inasmuch as more or fewer numbers of persons would meet with greater or lesser frequency.

Again we may look to Australia as a most striking instance of demographic determination of sociocentric terminology. There are great variations in the nature of food resources in Australia. In the coastal regions high rainfall creates such an amount, variety, and security of food that people live in large, relatively stable bands which are demographically close to each other. In the extremely arid interior, the people are scattered very thinly over the landscape during the long periods of drought. When it does rain, however, the desert is transformed and periods of relative abundance follow; then large numbers of people foregather for the great ceremonies, the *corrobborees*.

These infrequent but large meetings necessitate the use of the more impersonal, sociocentric status terminology, inasmuch as relative strangers are brought together. Probably all people in the world have at least a few sociocentric status terms, of course, such as "we" and "they," "friend" and "enemy," and terms for language division and people of particular localities which sometimes function as status terms. In Central Australia, however, the basic generation and moiety distinctions have also been named and thus objectified sociocentrically. This is the famous Australian "class system." There are two-class systems which consist of names for the two halves of the intermarrying divisions, and there are other two-class systems which consist of names for the two adjacent generations. In Central Australia these two criteria, generation and moiety, have been combined to make a four-part system. This is the most widespread of the class systems in Australia. In a more limited central block is the eight-class system, which subdivides the four classes into eight by distinguishing first cross-cousins from second cross-cousins of any Ego in the opposite moiety; that is, the moieties are made into what Radcliffe-Brown called "semi-moieties." Sociocentric terminology of this sort is based, therefore, on the same important criteria of status as the egocentric kinship system, but is a useful substitute for it under conditions which make it difficult for relative strangers to remember (or invent) the more precise and personal egocentric statuses they might indirectly hold to each other calculated through relationship to other particular persons.[8] A. P. Elkin (1932), the outstanding authority on the Australians, put it this way:

> The meeting of tribes for ceremonial purposes, and nowadays, too, the mixing of members of different tribes in white employ, facilitates and encourages the spread of such systems of summarizing kinship. They are naturally of very great value at intertribal gatherings, enabling camping, social activities, and marriages to be readily arranged, whereas the labor of comparing and adjusting the actual relationship through kinship terms alone in different languages, would be a very difficult process indeed [p. 325].

COMPOSITE BANDS

The most important examples of composite bands in Steward's discussion of this type are the Canadian big-game hunters, the Algonkian-speaking Indians of the eastern subarctic, and the Athabaskans of the central and western subarctic. The Andamanese are considered as a special case. For the present discussion I have included them, and also the Yahgan, in the composite category. The Eskimo and the Basin Shoshone, whom Steward considered as anomalously family-level instead of bands, also will be discussed in the present section.

---

[8] The relation of habitat to variations in the Australian class systems has been elaborated in Service (1960a). See also Lee and Devore (1968), Meggitt (1968), Rose (1968), Yengoyan (1968).

The Algonkians

Steward (1955, Ch. 8) describes the Algonkian Indians as having large, loose, composite bands, as a result of dependence on migratory game in an area of low population density. Nuclear families, however, own their own fur-trapping grounds which they inherit from their fathers.

Leacock (1955, p. 34) has shown that in modern times marital residence modes in the Montagnais-Naskapi bands of Algonkian Indians are informal and expedient among those groups who are not now wholly committed to fur-trapping. Those more fully specialized as entrepreneurial trappers, however, became more clearly patrilineal as *families*. The whole band, on the other hand, remains agamous (without a marriage rule) and relatively functionless.

The economic specialization by landowning nuclear families and the lack of clear marriage modes result in increased significance of the family and a decrease in the significance of the band as a residential group. The stabilization of the family also has been "consciously and unconsciously encouraged by the trading post factors, the governmental representatives, and the missionaries" (Leacock, 1955, p. 34).

It is impossible to generalize about modern status systems among all of the Algonkians, so variable and unstable are they. There are bifurcate-merging systems, others bifurcated in one generation and not in another, and still others resembling English-European types.

Steward (1955) believes that the aboriginal social organization before the fur trade must have been composite:

> Among the Canadian Algonkians, the subsistence and land-owning unit has usually been the bilateral family in historic times. In aboriginal times, however, when hunting of large game, which ranges in herds far beyond the limits of the family trapping territories, was the principal subsistence activity, the multifamily, composite band was probably not only the politi-

cal unit but also the landowning subsistence and social unit [p. 145].

Steward apparently reaches this conclusion on the basis of theory alone, for he cites no evidence. In recent years there have been several interesting historical investigations into the early period. Kinietz (1940, p. 326) finds evidence that the Chippewa (sometimes called Ojibwa or Salteurs) practiced virilocal marriage between 1615 and 1760. Eggan (1955, p. 532), considering the researches of Hallowell, Flannery, and others, concludes that the Canadian Algonkians in aboriginal times had cross-cousin marriage and the "sociological equivalent" of a bifurcate-merging terminological system, which is to say that they were *not* composite.

The historical sources tell more definitely the story of how the coming of trading Europeans to Canada resulted in depopulation by disease, upheavals, increased warfare, and so on, which altered the social organization of the Indians into composite units of refugees. For example, Kinietz (1940, p. 319) says that the Chippewa (a large language grouping) met with such disasters that by 1670 they numbered only 150 persons. Hickerson (1960, p. 101) says, "By 1670 the organization of villages or bands on the basis of kinship was obsolete, and by 1680 territorial occupancy was fluid and based on the contingencies of the moment rather than on tradition." Hickerson (1960) presents archival evidence that the unorganized, unstable, *ad hoc* groupings of Indians after 1680 had not always been that way:

> But the post-trade fragmentalism resulted in a different kind of organization than that which had characterized the pretrade communities. All indications are that the pretrade local group affiliation had been based on kinship, actual or fictive, and on the common use of a traditional territory, the employment of fisheries and hunting grounds circumscribed and limited by custom and guaranteed by the tacit recognition of neighbors. Post-trade fragmentation occurred on the basis of exigency, often of momentary exigency . . . [p. 100].

The fur trade was for a long time nearly all-pervasive in Indian Canada. In more recent times, however, the decimation of the animals and the decline in market prices for furs resulted in a trade depression in many areas and some Indians were forced to resume a hunting-gathering existence in remote areas after having been for a long time part of the fur trade. Dunning (1959), who has done ethnological and historical research on such groups, points out that modern hunting-gathering Indians, including those in the most remote areas, should not be taken as survivals of aboriginal social life: "The documented history of the Ojibwa shows clearly their interdependent relationship with Europeans. From the seventeenth century on it would not be true to consider them as an aboriginal population" (p. 4).

If we cannot conclude with finality that the aboriginal Algonkians were typical patrilocal bands in all respects, it does make the best supposition.[9] And we do have two major conclusions that seem firm: (a) the historical evidence shows that the bands once had a social organization and structure that was not merely composite; and (b) the unorganized, fluid, composite band of more recent times is readily accounted for as a consequence of the coming of the Europeans.

---

[9] Since the above was written an unpublished monograph by Charles Hockett, which reconstructs the Proto Central-Algonkian language, has come to my attention. Hockett in summary says (personal communication):

Using the comparative method of linguistics on the kinship terms of the modern Central Algonquian languages, we can reconstruct some portion of the Proto Central Algonquian. In my opinion, this parent language could not have been spoken later than about 1500 years ago. The evidence points rather clearly—again, in my opinion—towards patrilocality, patrilineality, and cross-cousin marriage of the narrower sort (male ego with mother's brother's daughter).

The Athabaskans[10]

The Athabaskans resemble the Algonkians not only in having a loose confederation of families which form a large composite band, but also in that for many of them the fur trade had created an increased independence of the nuclear families. Those like the modern Chipewyan, who still sometimes hunt caribou, have large composite bands according to Steward (1955, p. 147), because of the collective nature of the hunt.

Marriage modes are typically those expected of a composite band. Marriage is prohibited with known consanguinal relatives but there is no bar to marriage within the band. Marital residence is, as it is among the Algonkians, of any expedient sort, virilocal, uxorilocal, or neolocal; that is, there are no residence rules at all (MacNeish, 1960, pp. 287–288).

The basic unit in the social structure is the nuclear family, which in turn has its closest social relationships with near relatives in a few other families. The band itself is sometimes quite large (over 200–300) and includes many families not recognized as relatives. Steward's idea that this band is explained by the collective hunting of caribou and musk oxen is difficult to uphold, however, for I can find no evidence that the band itself is normally the hunting group.

The status terminology of kinship attributed to these Athabaskans is usually, but with some discrepancies, the so-called "Mackenzie Basin Type" named by Leslie Spier (MacNeish, 1960, p. 279). The distinguishing feature of this

---

[10] This section does not consider all the Canadian Athabaskans, for those west of the Rockies and in Alaska were fishermen resembling the Northwest coast chiefdoms in many respects. The Sarsi in southern Canada were equestrian buffalo hunters and are not to be included either. The composite big-game hunters at issue are the following: Hare, Dogrib, Bear Lake, Yellowknife, Chipewyan, Mountain, Kaska, Slave, Sekani, and Beaver.

system is that siblings and all cousins are called by the same term, that is, there is no cross-parallel (or moiety) distinction among the cousins. This is to be expected, of course, because of the bar to marriage with known relatives; hence, the status term merely designates "relative of own generation."

The aboriginal social organization, however, was apparently quite different. Fathauer (1942, pp. 30–32) concludes, as did Curtis (1928), that the Chipewyan once practiced cross-cousin marriage, and he finds that the earlier kinship system was congruent with such a mode.[11]

June Helm MacNeish's historical research (1960) on Hare, Slave, and Chipewyan revealed certain adaptive trends in the terminological system which led her to conclude that the aboriginal system was our standard bifurcate-merging type so consistent with local exogamy and cross-cousin marriage. She also found evidences of earlier sororate, levirate, and brother-sister exchange in marriage.

The causes of the modern fluid, informal, composite band clearly lie in the initial shocks, depopulation, relocation, and other disturbances in the early contact period which produced refugee-like groups of unrelated families among the Indians even before the time of the American Revolutionary War. Depopulation owing to European diseases had the first and most devastating social effects. Samuel Hearne, one of the early Hudson's Bay Company explorers, reported that in one year, sometime before 1783, *nine-tenths* of the Chipewyan Indian population was wiped out by smallpox (Tyrell, 1934, p. 115), and there are reports of many other devastating epidemics (Tyrell, pp. xiv, 216; Mackenzie, 1802, pp. xiii, xiv, xvii).

Athabaskans who survived the early disasters became employees (or, more accurately, debt-peons) of European fur-

---

[11] Some of the striking equivalencies in kin terms were: father's sister = mother-in-law; mother's brother = father-in-law; sibling-in-law = cross-cousin; child-in-law = cross-nephew or cross-niece.

trading companies almost 200 years ago. The "peace of the market" has prevailed since the coming of Europeans to the subarctic, and bands as functional units have become mingled, indistinct, and unimportant. Before this, it is clear, warfare among unrelated groups had been an enormously important consideration[12] in causing firm residential entities, marriage alliances among them, and the formation of adult male sodalities for defense as well as hunting—all of which cause strong social divisions as well as bonds and militate against the kind of amorphous organization called "composite."

The Yahgan

The Yahgan, coastal "canoe-Indians" of Tierra del Fuego, were primarily gatherers, not hunters. The day-to-day subsistence food was shellfish, especially mussels; fish, sea mammals, and birds were also eaten.

The Yahgan recognized territorial residential bands but there was no rule of band exogamy. The marriage mode was virilocal but the exogamic rule prohibited marriage with recognized (thus near) relatives only, without reference to the band as a whole which included unrelated people.

The social structure was thus based on nuclear families, with the closest ties of these families only to those closely related, such as families of brothers. The band as a totality was mixed, amorphous, and merely a territorial unit. Apparently there were no sodalities other than initiated men (adult males of the band).

The Yahgan kinship system was congruent with the social structure. Like the modern composite Athabaskans, in Ego's own generation there were no cross-parallel distinc-

---

[12] See, for example, accounts of eighteenth-century explorations by Dobbs (1744), Hearne and Turnor (Tyrell, 1934), Henry (1809), Mackenzie (1802), Thompson (Tyrell, 1916).

tions; a single term was used for all siblings and cousins together. But because the nuclear family was the autonomous unit, having associations with others only irregularly at best, Ego's mother and father were distinguished from the other relatives of that generation, as were own children from nieces and nephews and other relatives of that generation.

Clearly the environmental circumstances were not the causes of the partial compositeness of Yahgan society. The bands were not forced to mingle and disperse or to lose track of their identity as bands by the exigencies of the food quest. All observers have stated that there was enough food to be found within the conventional boundaries. It would appear, rather, that as in other instances of prolonged contact of Indians with Europeans, depopulation might have had something to do with the situation.

Because of their coastal position the Yahgan were exposed to European disease-carriers much earlier than were the inland Ona hunters, who retained a patrilocal band at the time they were described. By 1884 the Yahgan numbered only one-third of their former population, and by 1886 only four hundred remained of an earlier population estimated at 2500 to 3000. By 1913 there were less than one hundred Yahgan, and the ethnographer Father Martin Gusinde, who wrote the standard work on the Yahgan, made his field study in 1919–1923, when there were few survivors.[13]

Gusinde used informants in his attempt to reconstruct the aboriginal social organization, but it seems clear the fundamental social changes had taken place too long ago. Reverend Thomas Bridges, the first European resident in Yahgan country, said in 1884: "The changes wrought by recent in-

---

[13] The above population figures are from Cooper (1946, p. 83). The citations of Gusinde that follow are from the translation of his *Die Yamana* in the Human Relations Area Files under "Yahgan." The quoted statements of Reverend Bridges are most accessible in this source.

fluences have pushed the dialect groups and circles of families, which hitherto were separated in their circumscribed local districts, closer and closer together. Since 1880 a particularly strong movement in this direction set in. . . . The Yahgan are now so much more coalesced that they form a single colony" (Gusinde, pp. 631–632).

Reverend Bridges made a few statements relevant to the question of the earlier Yahgan social organization. Band territoriality had been observed: "All these natives are known by the name of their several localities and are very minutely divided into small clans" (p. 630). Hyades, speaking of roughly the same period, is quoted by Gusinde (p. 632) as saying that the Yahgan "were formerly divided into tribes that were hostile or antipathetic to one another." Local exogamy was usual (p. 422) and also a suggestion that virilocality was practiced is contained in Reverend Bridges' statement: "Marriage with very distant clans was infrequent from the natural unwillingness of women to separate themselves so entirely from their own people" (pp. 422–423).

It does not seem unwarranted to conclude that the Yahgan social organization as we know it was in the same state of transition as was that of the Athabaskans and Algonkians following depopulation, but before their readaptation to the fur trade as individual families. The ultimate difference between Yahgan and the above Canadian Indians, therefore, must be that Yahgan social organization was described at a stage in its dissolution which the Canadian Indians underwent much earlier, so that these latter have been described after a long period of acculturation and reconstitution of a social organization now adapted to modern conditions.

The Andaman Islanders

The Negritos of the isolated Andaman Islands at the time they were described ethnographically lived in bands which remained within rather restricted territories: ". . . each

band tract afforded an ample variety of foods so that a mo-
tive for ranging over a wider territory was lacking" (Steward,
1955, p. 148). Movement within the band territory was seasonal; in the rainy season the people were able to remain in
one village for several months, and in the rest of the year
they migrated in traditional orbits.

As reported by Radcliffe-Brown, who visited the Andamanese in 1906–1908, the marriage custom was unclear. The
majority of marriages were between persons of different local groups; thus there was at least a tendency toward band
exogamy. There is a suggestion of possible virilocality
in Radcliffe-Brown's statement about infant betrothal:[14]
"When children are betrothed it is the rule for the girl to
be adopted by the boy's parents, at any rate for a time"
(1948, p. 72).

E. H. Man wrote on the Andamanese after an earlier stay
of eleven years (1869–1880), but made only a few notes on
marriage and none on marital residence. He said that marriage was prohibited with any known relative and that this
rule applied equally to those related merely by the custom
of adoption (1932, p. 58). Neither a man nor a woman could
marry into the family of their brothers- or sisters-in-law (p.
59). This custom would have the effect of increasing the
number of marriage alliances for any particular family, but
would also, of course, tend to obliterate or obscure a moiety
arrangement.

The status terminology of the Andamanese, as reported
later by Radcliffe-Brown, reflects the rather amorphous
character of the band. In contrast to most primitive peoples,
the Andamanese used personal names freely in address and
reference; in this sense, relationships were highly individualized and personal. The status terms of address were, logi-

---

[14] This form of adoption is not peculiar to the Andamanese. Gusinde
(1955, pp. 26–27) reports a similar custom among the Congo Pygmies
and says that its purpose is to cement relationships between bands.

cally enough, left unspecific, highly impersonal, inasmuch as generational distinctions and relative age in own generation were the only criteria used in addition to sex. It is likely, actually, that the terms of address were sociocentric only, rather than egocentric, and functioned much as titles or terms like "Sir" do in European society. The terms of reference, on the other hand, resembled those of the Eskimo in that the nuclear family was distinguished in each generation from the other collaterals, who were undifferentiated.

Inasmuch as food was plentiful and the bands remained territorial, their habitat cannot explain the apparent partial compositeness of Andamanese bands. Steward felt that the explanation must be that the frequency of adoptions confused band memberships and locality. However, there is plenty of evidence in Man's report (1932, esp. pp. 57, 58, 68) that the people did not lose track of relationships because of adoption, and furthermore marriage exogamy applied equally to adopted and own relatives, as noted above.

Our best information on the social organization is by Radcliffe-Brown, but he admits dissatisfaction with his attempt because of the disorganization caused by depopulation. The population was only 18 per cent of its former numbers. "The diminution of population has combined with other causes to alter considerably the mode of life of the islanders. *What were formerly distinct and often hostile communities are now merged together*" (1948, p. 19. Italics mine).

Radcliffe-Brown made an attempt to reconstruct the previous system from older informants, but could not possibly have succeeded. Man's period of residence was thirty-odd years earlier, but even then depopulation was already well advanced. Both Man and Radcliffe-Brown did their work on South Andaman, where the British penal colony had been established, and syphilis already had infected two-thirds of the whole population in Man's period of residence (footnote 2, pp. 15–16). The "tribe" (dialect group) with which

Man was most "intimate" was once about 1000 but was reduced to only 400 (p. 30). He said:

> . . . contact with civilization has been marked with the usual lamentable result of reducing the aboriginal population; indeed, the death-rate, among those within the area of our influence, during the past twenty years has so far exceeded the birth-rate, as to compel the belief that before many decades have passed, the race, at least that portion of it which inhabits Great Andaman, will be well-nigh extinct [p. 3].

The Andamanese situation and the social results are similar to those of the Yahgan. The food supply was sufficient and territories were observed, but unrelated people merged together in them so that marriage choices and residence customs did not correspond to territoriality any longer. The merging, as elsewhere, clearly seems to have been related to extreme depopulation on the one hand and to cessation of interband hostilities on the other—both results of the intrusion of civilization.

The Basin Shoshone Indians—Anomalous?

Shoshonean-speaking Indians in historic times occupied the huge steppe-desert-and-plateau area between the Wasatch and Rocky Mountains on the east and the Sierra Nevadas on the west. They are conventionally separated into large categories such as Utes, Northern and Southern Paiutes, and Western and Northern Shoshone.

Steward's field work among the reservation Indians during the 1930s led him to conclude that those Shoshoneans of the desert area who did not acquire the horse in historic times had been at a family level of organization.

> Among Western Shoshone and many of their Northern Paiute and Southern Paiute neighbors it was physically impossible for families to remain in one place for any considerable time or for more than a few families to remain in permanent associa-

tion. The outstanding sociopolitical units, consequently, were the biological family and the small winter village, consisting of a loose aggregate of families. Families comprising a village were often related. . . . [But they were also] frequently unrelated because the lack of a rigid rule of post-marital residence and frequent shift of residence for practical reasons had prevented the formation of unilateral groups or lineages [Steward, 1938, p. 257].

All of the important economic activities and many others as well were undertaken by the family, which was the only stable social and political unit. Interlocking and widely scattered subsistence areas prevented ownership of land by particular families, and associations of families for communal enterprises were expedient and temporary rather than consistent and structured.

It is, of course, admissible to call such groupings family level rather than bands. But the description corresponds to what we have been calling the composite band so far, hence to agree with Steward's usage would introduce semantic confusion at this point. Furthermore, most of the bands under survey here, including patrilocal bands like the central Australians, are composed of nuclear family units that themselves undertake most of the economic tasks. The families are rarely all together in a total meeting of the band or bands. The big difference in any of these bands is whether reciprocal exogamy between groups or sodalities and virilocal residence rules are operative; this is what determines whether several nuclear families, *scattered or not,* are a structured band of families or are at a family level, with the larger society being merely informal, haphazard, and ad hoc.

In order to discuss the aboriginal state of affairs it is practical to think of two different areas and times. The southern half of the Great Basin area was explored at an earlier date (the first reports beginning in 1776) than was the Great Salt Lake route to Oregon and California, first reported by Lewis and Clark in 1805. The earlier date of European reports on the Southern Paiute and southern groups of Western Shoshone is very important, for we have information that antedates the use of horses by these Indians, whereas for the Northern Paiute, and the Northern and Western Shoshone, the situation at the time of the earliest accounts was greatly complicated by the warfare and dislocations caused by mounted predatory Indians who resembled some of those of the Great Plains.

The Southern Paiute were met and described at early dates by Escalante, Garcés, Potts, Armijo, and Ogden. According to Buckles' (1960) summary of these sources, none of the Indians observed had as yet been subjugated or preyed upon by mounted Indians. There was strong localism, and most of the explorers recorded the different groups as *bands* residing in particular areas. The Indians that Escalante talked to were conscious of their territorial limits and were "fearful to exceed them" (Bolton, 1950, pp. 203, 206–208, 213, 216–217). Escalante also noted slight and gradual language changes from area to area, which suggests that the Indians had not been disturbed for a long time (Bolton, pp. 204, 226–227). Garcés described a similar situation among Southern Paiute in the Mohave Desert (Coues, 1900, pp. 243–245). On the other hand, the Ute Indians encountered in north central Utah were already being pressured by mounted Shoshones from the north.

The northern groups were contacted by Lewis and Clark in 1805, after which large numbers of trappers, traders, and wagon trains passed through the area. American fur companies and the Northwest Company contended for the area's resources, particularly in the Snake River system, and probably had some considerable effect on the Indians.

The Shoshoneans in the northern basin-plateau area in the early 1800s were of two main types, though known under a wide variety of names. There were mounted Indians who hunted buffalo in some seasons, fished in others, and monopolized the more fertile areas as pastures for their horses. They were grandly dominant over the other Indians, whom they scattered widely in small units and denied access to fishing sites and good hunting and gathering areas. Both groups, however, were in turn preyed upon by Blackfoot and Piegan horsemen from the north.

The dominated horseless Indians and the equestrian Indians originally were probably alike, but after some acquired horses, the others were pushed into such poor areas that their lot worsened terribly, and they were almost always described as beggarly, thieving, starving, and miserable in contrast to their proud cousins, the Utes and Northern Shoshone, whose original culture was altered in the other direction, toward true tribal organization.

If the horseless Indians could steal horses they ate them, having no alternative. One "Ban-at-tee" (probably Northern Paiute) said to Alexander Ross in 1824, "We can never venture into the open plains for fear of the Blackfoot and Piegans, and for that reason never keep horses" (Ross, 1956, p. 176). In 1825, Ross captured a lone Ban-at-tee who explained that his people had to live scattered and in hiding because "were we to live in large bands, we should easily be discovered" (pp. 277–278).

In the more central parts of the Great Basin, the foot Indians may have been less preyed upon,[15] but in 1857 the great Comstock Lode was discovered at Virginia City:

> Within 10 years prospectors penetrated the remotest parts of the territory and boom towns sprang up in the midst of sheer desert. Shoshoni, who had previously had little contact with the white man, congregated at many of these towns. Meanwhile, immigrants had begun to settle at oases in the desert and soon

---

[15] The mounted Ute of western Utah used to hunt the Nevada "diggers" in the spring of the year, however, when they were weak from a winter of hunger, and fatten them for sale at slave markets in Santa Fe, New Mexico (Farnham, quoted in Steward, 1938, p. 9); further discussion in Service (1970, Ch. 10).

live stock grazed the hills, decimating native food plants, and white men cut down pinyon trees for fuel [Steward, 1938, p. 7].

The earliest scientific description (as distinct from travelers' accounts) of the Western Shoshone was by Major Powell and his assistant, Ingalls, in 1872. First they describe the consequences of white occupation.

With respect to Paiutes: "Their hunting grounds have been spoiled, their favorite valleys are occupied by white men, and they are compelled to scatter in small bands in order to obtain subsistence" (Powell and Ingalls, 1874, p. 3).

With respect to Shoshones of central Nevada: "[They] are in an exceedingly demoralized state; they prowl about the mining camps, begging and pilfering, the women prostituting themselves to the lust of the lower class of men. There are no Indians in all of the territory . . . whose removal [to reservations] is so imperatively demanded by considerations of justice and humanity, as those Shoshones of Nevada" (p. 21).

Powell and Ingalls calculated that their original population had been 1945, divided into thirty-one tribes (p. 20), which, interestingly enough, averages sixty-three persons per group—a fairly standard band size elsewhere in the world.

> The original political organization of the tribes under consideration had a territorial basis; that is, the country was divided into districts, and each district was inhabited by a small tribe, which took the name of the land, and had one principal chief. These tribes, or "land-nameds," as they are called in the Indian idiom, were the only permanent organizations, but sometimes two or more of them would unite in a confederacy under some great chief [p. 9].

Steward takes a view contrary to that of Powell. It is difficult to see, however, why a man so famous for scientific rectitude and painstaking attention to detail as was Powell (who founded the Bureau of American Ethnology) should have reported "small tribes" (it is apparent by context that

he means "kinship units" by this word) named for their territories had they not once existed, and, we may ask, how
could the Indians have described them? And as we have
seen, there is earlier documentary confirmation of this organization for the southern part of the Great Basin area.
There is no way of knowing precisely what the aboriginal
kinship terminology and marital residence rules were, of
course, but it is suggestive at least that Steward's ethnographic account (1938) of the Basin Shoshone reveals that
many of them retained cross-cousin marriage customs, sororate and levirate, and bifurcate-merging terminology in
Ego's adjacent generations. In Ego's own generation terms
are variable, as might be expected, because this is the level
at which changes in marriage customs are immediately felt.
(The Yahgan are similar in this.) If one believes that terminological patterns are functionally consistent with social
structure, then the bifurcate-merging characteristics may be
survivals of an earlier form of patrilocal band organization.
There seems to be no other way to explain them.[16]

The Eskimo—Anomalous?

Except for certain Alaskan groups which have patrilineal
(patrilocal?) lineages and cross-cousin marriage (Hughes,
1958), the Eskimo have in historic times been described as
remarkably alike in their fluid, open communities which
lack territorial exogamy and associated rules of marital residence. The individual nuclear households are the basic economic units, and as they move with the seasons to various
hunting and fishing grounds they may peacefully join others

---

[16] Steward is aware of the disconformity of the terminological patterns
with the disorganized situation which he believes was aboriginal. He
concludes that kinship therefore is *not* functionally related to social
organization: "In short, historic, linguistic, and psychological factors
as well as functional necessity have combined in different ways to
produce the terms" [1938, p. 285].

in any of those places, whether they are related or not. That is, any villages or camp units are composite.

Because the lack of local exogamy and rules or customs of unilocal residence leaves a nuclear household with only ephemeral social relations with others, the kinship terminology normally separates the persons of the nuclear family from all other relatives except parents' siblings. The other relatives in turn are differentiated merely by sex and generation.[17]

The question of whether this was the aboriginal Eskimo organization is a difficult one. There are no "survivals" in the usual kinship terminology (unless in Alaska) that point to a different earlier organization; hence either that organization was the same as the one today, or the changes occurred so long ago that a complete functional reorganization was possible. The first suspicion is that the present compositeness of Eskimo society was caused by depopulation and other disruptions and catastrophies contingent upon the coming of Europeans, simply because we have seen these as causes of the composite band in other areas.

The famous authority on the arctic, Vilhjalmur Stefansson, in his *Encyclopaedia Britannica* article, "Eskimos" (1927, p. 708) says:

It is difficult to estimate what the population may have been before the white man came. Contagious diseases, introduced by Europeans, notably measles, have wrought great havoc among the Canadian and Alaskan Eskimos. In certain western districts a single epidemic about a quarter of a century ago is known to have killed from 25% to 75% in different places. Judging from Richardson's account there must have been more than a thou-

---

[17] The above passages have been criticized by David Damas (personal communication) as oversimple and too generalized. His work among Eskimos suggests much more variation in group composition and in kinship terminology than has been believed. It should be expected, of course, that various kinds and degrees of reconstitution have been occurring and will continue.

sand Eskimos in the Mackenzie Delta in 1848, and perhaps twice
that number. But in 1906 Stefansson found these represented
by less than thirty descendants. Fully half of that reduction appeared to be accounted for by two epidemics within the memory of people who were still living in 1906, and the preceding
reduction was doubtless due to epidemics then forgotten, perhaps one or more of the smallpox plagues that have swept
aboriginal Canada. Similar reductions in numbers seem likely
for all sections except Greenland. Even there epidemics doubtless took toll formerly, but a strict quarantine maintained by
the Danes has enabled the population to increase considerably
during the last half century. Perhaps 100,000 may be a reasonable minimum estimate for Eskimo numbers before white contact began to injure as well as benefit the natives.

One of the earliest of the scientific accounts of the Eskimo
was Boas' (1888) description of the Central Eskimo. He was
not concerned with either social organization or acculturation but rather with geography and Eskimo material culture, yet he frequently refers to the profound alterations in
Eskimo society caused by European diseases, use of firearms,
and the continuing presence of whalers of all nations during the great nineteenth-century boom which culminated
in the disappearance of whales from the vicinity of the Central Eskimo even before he arrived.

During the last decades the most important inducement to
removals [of people from their natal territories] has been the
presence of whalers in certain parts of the country. Since the
beginning of our century [the nineteenth] their fleets have visited the west shore of Baffin Bay and Davis Strait, and thus
European manufactures have found their way to the inhospita-
ble shores of the Arctic Sea. . . .
When the whalers became better acquainted with the natives
and the peculiar jargon which is still in use was developed, the
traffic became very active. . . . As soon as the whalers began to
winter in the sound and to employ the natives the latter received firearms and European boats in exchange for their wares,
and then their modes of living became materially changed. The
immense quantity of European manufactured articles which
thus came into the possession of the natives induced the re-

moval of many families to the favored region [Boas, 1888, p. 466].

Other tribes sold skins to whalers in Cumberland Sound and spent the winter there for the rations given by the traders. "The constant contact between the Eskimo and the whalers has effected a perfect revolution in the trade between the Eskimo tribes. As the whale catch in Cumberland Sound has fallen off during the past fifteen years, a remigration of the population of Davis Strait has occurred, ships visiting those shores every fall and a regular traffic being kept up" (p. 468). Firearms had become plentiful and a great many tribes engaged in the fur trade (pp. 468–469). As the whaling fell off, the whaling stations continued to stay on by engaging in trade for seal blubber and skins (p. 467). Other, more inland Eskimos, traded with the Hudson's Bay Company at Fort Churchill (p. 450).

There were a number of important indirect consequences of the coming of the Europeans. The Eskimos formerly were active whale hunters, and "a single capture supplied them with food for a long time," but the whaling was "yielded up to the Europeans and Americans" (p. 440). Walrus had also once been abundant at Cumberland Sound, but had diminished greatly (p. 438).

In addition to the loss in food supplies there had been a drastic depopulation due to disease. "When the whalers first visited Cumberland Sound, the population may have amounted to 1,500 . . . Since [1840] the population has diminished at a terrible rate. In 1857 Warmow . . . estimated it at 300 . . ." (p. 425). "The reason for the rapid diminution of the population of this country is undoubtedly to be found in the diseases which have been taken thither by the whalers." Syphilis had been the worst killer, but Boas also mentions diphtheria and pneumonia as common (p. 426).

It has been noted that a frequent consequence of depopulation is the fluid merging and mingling of previously unrelated groups. Boas says: "Formerly, the Oqomiut were divided into four subtribes [they were named by their territories, which Boas describes] . . . their old settlements are still inhabited, but their separate tribal identity is gone, a fact which is due as well to the diminution in their numbers as to the influence of the whalers visiting them" (pp. 424–425).

A similar situation is described for another locality, Nettilling Fjord. "It is probable that the high mortality of recent years has induced the Eskimo to band together more closely than they formerly did and to adopt the plan of returning to Nettilling Fjord at the beginning of winter" (p. 433). The effects of depopulation in the high arctic are exactly the same that we have seen in the coasts, desert, or rain forest: the loss of integrity of the localized kinship bands and a merging of the survivors into expedient composite groups.

The Copper Eskimo farther west were not affected by the fur trade and presence of Europeans at such an early date as the Central Eskimo were. They had been contacted as early as 1770 by Samuel Hearne, but apparently not as yet directly influenced by European manufactures when Stefansson visited them in 1908–1912. Indirect influence, however, particularly depopulation, had resulted in the same merging of surviving unrelated peoples that Boas had noted farther east.

First of all, as we might expect, Stefansson found many evidences of a formerly greater population in the area. For example: ". . . there is little doubt that there was a continuous chain of habitations prior to say 1830, all the way east along the coast from Langton Bay to Coronation Gulf . . ." (1919, p. 25). Again: "at two times many of the people around Langton Bay died, the first time of starvation; the second time of an epidemic" (p. 303). Stefansson calculates that this had occurred fifteen years before his visit; the survivors split into three groups, "because they had become so few," and went in different directions to join other people. There are references to a great measles epidemic in 1900 in the Mackenzie region which could have caught the neighboring Copper Eskimo (p. 24). The Copper Eskimo, it might be noted, went on long trading expeditions, even as far east as Chesterfield Inlet where they met "Eskimo who deal with the white men of Hudson Bay" (p. 113). There had been a steady decrease in the number of caribou in recent years (p. 78). Whaling was no longer practiced but there was much evidence that "whaling must have been one of the industries of this entire district" (p. 18).

Stefansson did not describe the social organization or marriage customs of the Copper Eskimo in any coherent way, which may have been because there were no coherent rules. Virilocality was observed in the cases of Indian-Eskimo marriages (Stefansson, 1919, p. 15), however.

Stefansson is fully aware of the problem of being too late to observe the aboriginal Eskimo culture, and is also aware of the fact that what may have happened is *de*culturative loss even before positive acculturation, or borrowing, takes place. In one interesting passage in his journal (1914, p. 323), titled "Importance of Early Ethnographical Work," he describes how Petitot's *Monographie* gives an "excellent" counting system which the present descendants of Petitot's informants had entirely forgotten. In another brief item in his journals, Stefansson remarks on the influence of Alaskans and whites in altering Eskimo customs in the use of personal names. Among the groups least influenced by Westerners the custom of teknonymy was in force, and there was a general taboo of the use of personal names (1914, pp. 365–366). (I have long held a theory, as yet not well tested: the use of personal names or nicknames instead of kinship terms in a primitive culture might be a product of deculturation and shattered social organization.)

Stefansson gives an enlightening account of the actual

creation of a composite group by the typical depopulation and merging process. In 1880 the Eskimo village at Cape Smyth on the Arctic coast contained 400 people. In 1910, at the time of Stefansson's visit, the population was the same—*but* only four of those Eskimos were descendants of the original Cape Smyth tribe! The death rate had been so great that nearly everyone of the village had been wiped out, but the whaling at Cape Smyth was so prosperous that driblets of immigrants kept coming in from a dozen or more other decimated communities (1919, p. 66).

The most instructive of all of the early monographs is that of Holm (in Thalbitzer, 1914), who studied the Ammassalik of the east Greenland coast in 1883–1885, whose community had never been visited by Europeans. Their isolation was caused by the Europeans' lack of access to the region by ship because of the nearness of the ice pack (Holm's party arrived by umiak).

The social organization of the Ammassalik presents quite a different appearance from that of the modern Canadian Eskimo. Their subsistence habits were similar to those of coastal Eskimos elsewhere in that they maintained winter settlements in one place, largely for the sealing, and scattered elsewhere in the summer for fishing and hunting. But the Ammassalik society was a structured one, despite the seasonal variation in food supplies. The population of Ammassalik Fjord was 413 in 1884, divided into thirteen patrilocal "longhouses" scattered individually in different parts of the fjord (Thalbitzer, 1914, p. 185). This gives an average of thirty-two people per longhouse, but some were apparently larger: "In one house half a score of families, and several generations of each family, may be accommodated. Each house is under the rule of a head or chief; this function devolves on the eldest man, when he either is a skillful hunter himself, or has been so in the past and now has sons who have inherited his ability" (p. 57).

Marriage was locally exogamous by longhouse community, virilocal, and kinship ties extended far beyond the immediate nuclear family, though affinal ties were not strong. (Unfortunately, Holm gives no good information on kin terminology.)

> The family tie, that is to say the tie of blood, is regarded as an obligation to stand by one another under all circumstances. Marriage is not regarded as a family tie.
>
> Thus, whereas relationship in the third and fourth degree is respected, the wife is regarded merely in the light of a mistress or a servant from whom the husband can part whenever he chooses. When she has borne a child, however, her position becomes securer.
>
> As is only right and proper, the husband is the chief person in the family; next after him come the sons, even if they are quite small children: they will one day become hunters and support their parents in their old age. As long as the parents are alive, most of the sons live with them and contribute to their support. However, in some cases, where there are many sons, the younger ones go and live with the families of their wives [pp. 59–60].

The people of Ammassalik Fjord were largely endogamous as a scattered community. They were, of course, distant from others and a large enough population to form a marriage isolate. The group was therefore composite in one sense of the word, when we refer to the whole, but it was not unstructured, or disorganized, with fluid ad hoc membership in the sense in which composite has been used so far. And even when longhouse virilocality was violated in some cases, it was because of a preponderance of males, as can happen in any system of bands of small size (like those of central Australia, for example); it was not a mere response to local food supplies.

Holm's visit to the Ammassalik led to the founding of a Danish trading-missionary station there in 1894. Thalbitzer's later description (pp. 347–348) referring to the people subsequent to 1894 is interesting because it shows how altered our understanding of Ammassalik social organization would be had Holm not arrived prior to the coming of this single trading station.

In 1895, ten years after Holm's visit (and one year after the post was established) the population of Ammassalik Fjord, which had been 413, was reduced to only 247. Later, people from elsewhere joined the community and the population increased (pp. 348–349), with the typical merging that we have noted elsewhere. Thalbitzer's most succinct statement of the situation is as follows:

> When the summer hunting is over, the families return to the winter settlements, not at one time, but gradually. The same families do not live in the same house each winter and the composition of the settlement changes from year to year. Often new arrangements are made at the summer meetings on the common hunting grounds, without very much attention being paid to family relationships and constant exchanges may occur. But this possibly springs from newer tendencies in this tribe. The constant uncertainty of the hunting in recent years has often led, it may be, to an increasing disposition to try new hunting grounds. Originally the relationship was most probably the basal principle in deciding the winter groups [p. 347].

It seems clearly evident that aboriginal Eskimo society was not fluid, informal, and composite, nor was it a family level of integration caused by the nature of the game hunted. The later composite groups of unrelated Eskimo known to modern ethnology are readily explained as a consequence of direct and indirect European influences that can only be described as catastrophic.

It would probably be unwarranted to argue that the precontact social organization of the Eskimo generally had to be like that of the Ammassalik, but the data on that group are certainly suggestive, particularly when combined with Boas' findings of earlier, more organized "subtribes" based on territoriality among the Central Eskimo and Stefansson's accounts of the creation of composite communities by merging in other areas to the west.

THE BAND LEVEL OF SOCIOCULTURAL INTEGRATION

The simplest, most rudimentary form of social structure, as a *structure* (thus excluding fortuitous or expedient groupings of the refugee and composite sort), is the patrilocal band. For this reason alone it could be scientifically assumed to be the earliest as well. It also seems to be the most practical form for foraging peoples who are below the demographic level of tribal villages.

It is truly an important, even astonishing, fact that we find this social structure in all the major quarters of the earth and in such tremendously varying habitats as deserts, seacoasts, plains, and jungles, in tropical, polar, and temperate zones, with great variations in kinds and amounts of food, and with seasonal and yearly alterations in the supplies. This is an even better reason for thinking that the patrilocal band is early; it seems almost an inevitable kind of organization.

The composite band, on the other hand, is obviously a product of the near-destruction of aboriginal bands after contact with civilization. In all cases, there is conclusive evidence of rapid depopulation by disease which, when combined with the ending of hostilities among the aborigines themselves under the dominance of the common enemy, resulted in the merging of previously unrelated peoples.[18] Evidence that the bands were patrilocal before disaster struck was not conclusive in every case, but there was enough indirect evidence to make it the best supposition. Certainly conclusive, however, is the fact that variations in

---

[18] And on the other hand, many kinds of foraging bands described in modern times, notably in South America, are simply "devolved" remnants of former larger tribal-horticultural societies, some of which retained matrilineal or matrilocal features of social organizations (Martin, 1969).

geographical adaptation has nothing whatsoever to do with preventing or *frustrating* the formation of the patrilocal band. Finally, it is of great interest that in their general characteristics bands are very much alike, no matter their habitat, race, language, or the quarter of the globe in which they are found.

From the point of view of cultural evolution this rudimentary society could be called, adopting Steward's phraseology, the Band Level of Sociocultural Integration. With this phrase it is possible to go somewhat beyond social organization as such and to use the basic social features to characterize and name the whole culture as a type. The salient feature of the type is simply that all of the functions of the culture are organized, practiced, or partaken of by no more than a few associated bands made up of related nuclear families. The economy, for example, is organized by and takes place entirely within these units: there are no special economic groups or special productive units such as guilds or factories, no specialized occupational groups, no economic institutions such as markets, no special consuming groups or classes. The economy, in short, is not separately institutionalized, but remains merely an aspect of kinship organization; in the usual modern sense of the word, there is no formal economy at all.

The same is true of other cultural functions. There is no separate political life and no government or legal system above the modest informal authority of family heads and ephemeral leaders. Likewise, there is no religious organization standing apart from family and band; and the congregation is the camp itself.

The fact that family and band are simultaneously the sole economic, political, and religious organization greatly influences the character of these activities. The economy, polity, and ideology of the culture of bands is unprofessionalized and unformalized; in short, it is familistic only.

4

The Social Organization of Tribes

It may be supposed that there were instances of the tribal level of society in the paleolithic era. But inasmuch as these were still hunters and gatherers, they remained closely dependent on nature even though they occupied areas permitting relatively high productivity. These areas must have been niches, so to speak, with an unusual juxtaposition of several resources, such that the tribal societies attained this level only in certain places and could not exert dominance widely. They could be considered cases of specific rather than general dominance.

The neolithic revolution based on the domestication of plants and animals, on the other hand, permitted a much more effective control over the natural environment than simple foraging and could be effective in more environments. The instances of tribal level attained on this technological base could therefore exert general dominance and thus must have spread widely at the expense of foraging bands. Of course there still remained enormous areas where plant and animal domestication was not effective, or which remained isolated from neolithic influences by geographic

barriers. Thus neolithic societies came to coexist with paleolithic societies in time but not in space.

As tribal society became more generally dominant it also
became more specifically diversified. As the new economy
adapted itself to varying local circumstances a number of
different kinds of tribes came into being. Tribal society
thus has general characteristics as a level or stage in evolution and, at the same time, several specific variants which
arose by adaptation and specialization and survived into
nearly modern times.

THE RISE OF TRIBAL SOCIETY

The evolution of culture as measured by changes in social
structure consists of a movement in the direction of greater
size and density of the social body, an increase in the number
of groups, greater specialization in the function of groups,
and new means of integrating the groups.

A band is only an association, more or less residential, of
nuclear families, ordinarily numbering twenty-five to one
hundred people, with affinal ties allying it with one or a few
other bands. A tribe is an association of a much larger number of kinship segments which are each composed of families. They are tied more firmly together than are the bands,
which use mostly marriage ties alone. A tribe is of the order
of a large collection of bands, but it is not *simply* a collection of bands. The ties that bind a tribe are more complicated than those of bands and, as we shall see, the residential
segments themselves come to be rather different from bands.
Also, it should not be implied that tribes necessarily arise
through growth and segmentation; probably there were a
number of specific routes to tribalism. The important point
is that the few intermarrying multifamily local groups that
were the whole of band society are now only a part or as-

pect of tribal society, and are in some measure transformed by that factor.

If the primary local kin segments of tribal society are no longer mere bands, and if they are specifically variable under different conditions of adaptation, then it follows that their divergences among themselves and their general distinctiveness as compared to bands must arise from some causes *outside* themselves, from the adaptive circumstances which select for rules and resulting institutions that are tribal-wide. Here again is an opportunity to try out the prescription announced in the Introduction: proceed from external environment in its wider sense to see what rules have created what sodalities and groups, and then follow with an analysis of resultant smaller segments, families, and interpersonal relations and statuses.

It may be stipulated that domesticated plants and/or animals made possible (though they did not *cause*) a much higher level of economic productivity and, importantly, a much more stable, consistent productivity than at the hunting-gathering level. Much larger aggregations of people were possible, therefore, and in much reduced territory. It may be presumed also that these aggregations retained elements of the social organization that they had had at the band level, local exogamous groups allied by affinal ties. Once these residential groups are larger and there are more of them, however, problems of consolidation of the whole exist, and a tribe is not formed until such consolidation takes place. There is nothing in this demographic situation alone which would necessarily lead to a tribal form of organization; probably the earliest growing societies simply divided and spread. With competition, however, the larger and better consolidated would prevail, other things equal. Here again external offense-defense requirements may well have been the selective factors, signifying as they do the importance of alliance and solidarity.

Bandlike modes of exogamy and marital residence cannot do the job of holding a larger society together, for the alliances formed by such reciprocity become increasingly diffuse as the number of residential groups increases. And tribes are not held together by the dominance of one group over others, nor are there any other true or permanent political-governmental institutions. Presumably a great many societies of tribal potentiality merely fissioned, but those that became tribes all had made certain social inventions that had latent integrating effects. To ask what these are is to ask what a tribe is.

The means of solidarity that are specifically tribal additions to the persisting bandlike means might be called *pantribal sodalities.* As we have seen, sodalities sometimes exist in band society under special circumstances, but they are few and limited in scope, that is, they are not pan-tribal. Probably the most usual of pan-tribal sodalities are clans, followed by age-grade associations, secret societies, and sodalities for such special purposes as curing, warfare, ceremonies, and so on. These institutions were all foreshadowed to an extent—they are made out of ingredients that existed in band society—but they are now transformed in certain ways. Why these come about and in what form, however, depended on the adaptive circumstances.[1]

These adaptive circumstances—the environment—can be seen as having two aspects, each of which can vary independently of the other in relative importance. They are (a) the natural (organic and inorganic) environment and (b) the presence of competing societies, the superorganic environment. The natural habitat has received attention from anthropologists in studies of cultural ecology, but the superorganic aspect of environment has not had nearly enough study. Hence we may appropriately begin with a brief dis-

---

[1] See Sahlins (1968) for a discussion of the characteristics of tribal society as a stage in general cultural evolution.

cussion of this factor. It will be considered only generally in this section and more specifically later when we consider certain prominent adaptive variations in tribal social organization.

The competition of societies in the neolithic phase of cultural development seems to have been the general factor which led to the development of integrating pan-tribal sodalities. The kind of natural habitat is important, of course, in a consideration of the size, stability, and number of residential groups and the general density of population in an area, but problems arising from this kind of adaptation are technological and economic, not political. It seems likely that without foreign-political problems overall tribal integration would not take place; it is always such problems that stimuate the formation of larger political bodies.

Band society, out of which tribes grew, was egalitarian except for certain personal inequalities in the familistic statuses such as young-old, male-female. The egalitarian nature of society, the lack of political hierarchies and dominant groups, continues in tribal society. Leadership is personal—charismatic—and for special purposes only in tribal society; there are no political offices containing real power, and a "chief" is merely a man of influence, a sort of adviser. The means of tribal consolidation for collective action are therefore not governmental. And once the means are in effect the tribe is largely self-regulating, in contrast to higher levels of polity which, though in important measures self-regulating, are also *regulated by* persons institutionalized for that purpose.

Thus a tribe is a fragile social body compared to a chiefdom or a state. It is composed of economically self-sufficient residential groups which because of the absence of higher authority take unto themselves the private right to protect themselves. Wrongs to individuals are punished by the corporate group, the "legal person." Disputes in tribal society tend to generate feuds between groups. The feud is the greatest source of disunity and disruption to any ungoverned society, for feuds tend to perpetuate themselves, with each act of revenge typically generating a corresponding reprisal.

Considering the lack of institutional political means of unity and the absence of organic solidarity, and considering such grave sources of disunity as feuds, it seems remarkable that a tribe remains a tribe. It seems sensible to reaffirm that *external* strife and competition *among* tribes must be the factor that provides the necessity for internal unity.

The external polity of tribes is usually military only. Usually, too, the military posture is consistently held; that is, a state of war or near-war between neighboring tribes is nearly perpetual. Tribal warfare by its nature is inconclusive. Ambush and hit-and-run raids are the tactics rather than all-out campaigns, which cannot of course be economically sustained by a tribal economy and its weak organization. True conquest, furthermore, would be self-defeating, for the productivity of a defeated tribe would not be great enough to sustain the conquerors. Objectives seem to be booty (as in the raiding for cattle and horses among pastoralists) or to drive the enemy out of a favored zone or prevent him from expanding (the characteristic objectives of war among horticulturalists). But territory is not easily taken and held in the absence of decisive engagements. Continual threat, sniping, and terrorization which will discourage and harass the enemy is the typical form of action. In fact, terrorization, or psychological warfare, seems to be at its highest development in tribal society. Headhunting, cannibalism, torture of prisoners, rape, massacre, and other forms of atrocious nerve-warfare are probably more effective means to the end at the tribal level than is true combat.

At any rate, the bellicose state of intertribal relations tends to be unremitting and is thus a strong environmental inducement for a consistent unity of the various independent tribal segments or local kin groups. The means at hand for making a larger entity, a "people," however, are nothing more than the familistic bonds and small sodalities of band society.

It is apparent that the problems of unity were met in the extension of sodalities. Pan-tribal sodalities make a tribe a tribe, for if they did not exist then there is nothing but a series of bands, more affluent than hunters and gatherers but still bands, with only intermarriage between certain ones providing any unity. To put it another way: the development of pan-tribal sodalities is the emergent feature which made bands over into a new level of sociocultural integration and thus a new cultural type.

Pan-tribal sodalities may be divided into two basic kinds, those which are derived from the kinship order and those which are not. Kinship sodalities are ordinarily of three types: the clan, the kindred, and the rarer segmentary lineage; non-kinship sodalities include such associations as age-grades, and warrior and ceremonial societies.

All of these were to some degree prefigured in band society. Clans, segmentary lineages, and kindreds are modeled after the family, the vertical solidary unit, in their basic character. Warrior societies, age-grades, and the like have their prototypes in the horizontal solidary units— the "brothers," the "old men," and the cooperative hunting and ceremonial groups. But one obvious and apparently simple but very important thing had to be done to make these ingredients over into large pan-tribal sodalities. They had to be maintained on a nonlocal basis. Here again, as in the "invention" of rules of marriage and residence which created band society, new cultural elements had to be added.

First of all and most obviously, a pan-tribal sodality, because it is not local, must have a name. A patrilineal clan, for example, is like a patrilocal band in that it is exogamous and membership is from birth, from father to child. But a patrilocal band is residential and its membership is only de facto a matter of descent. It is in fact made up of patrilineally descended persons, but this is an accident, a by-product of the mode of residence. A clan, however, is not a residential group; most of the time it is not a group of any kind, for it cross-cuts groups. Membership is no longer in terms of place (of birth or residence), hence a clan needs a name which is not territorial. It needs the concept of descent, of common ancestry. Special insignia and ceremonies are also strengthening factors. It should be emphasized that the clan's concept of descent is not yet necessarily a conception of *genealogical* descent; it is merely the idea of common descent from a putative ancestor. To emphasize the fact that the conception of descent in clans is not genealogical we should note that clan members do not, unless they are in fact close, recently separated relatives, trace any specific genealogical connections among themselves. Often the original ancestor is not even thought of as a human being, but is a totemic plant or animal.[2]

Thus a clan is not merely a patrilocal band or extended family which has grown and become dispersed over the tribal domain, although such growth is the likely precondition for the birth of clanship. There are many instances of dispersion and fissioning of bands or lineages in the ethnographic literature. They do not become clans unless external conditions make it desirable—if not necessary—for the once-contiguous group of people to maintain their sense of alliance, of cooperation, of corporateness for certain purposes such as defensive alliance and food-sharing. Then they create a name, insignia, ceremony, mythology of descent, clan history, and so on. However simple such an in-

---

[2] This is not to say that genealogical relationships *cannot* be traced —or thought of—between any two relatives in a clan, but rather that it is not normal to do so, given the social functions of clan sodalities. It might even be improper: for example, Beattie shows that Nyoro clan members consider it wrong to make a distinction between close and distant kin in the clan, such as between "real brothers" and "clan brothers." A clan should be solidary throughout its membership and not in conflict as a result of loyalties to various family units (Beattie, 1957–1958).

vention as a name for a clan or the idea of common descent
may be, it would seem that such social inventions are not
without a reason, without relation to circumstances. This
is not to say, of course, that members of a clan set about to
create a pan-tribal institution which serves to integrate the
society when they name themselves and try to perpetuate
their association in various other ways. Far from that; it is
probable that they were thinking of themselves only. But
this institution made them strong and others, faced with it,
would in time be likely to create their own. Here again it
may be suggested, speculatively, that such short-term interests persisted because finally they came to serve long-term
interests of the whole society. The clan, as a pan-tribal
sodality, is in this view a probable development of a growing, fissioning society under certain circumstances. And we
do find, in fact, that clans are typically associated with tribes
whose kin groups are, or had been, of the unilocal—later,
lineal—type.[3]

The diversity of sodalities among ethnologically known
tribes is matched by a great range in kinds of residential
groups. The number of possible kinds of social structures
at the tribal level seems greater than at the band level. Possibly this impression of greater diversification is simply because there are more tribes than bands known to us in modern times. However, it seems probable also that the neolithic
developments made more kinds of natural environment
exploitable in more kinds of ways. In tribal economy there
are varying emphases and combinations of agriculture, pastoralism, hunting, fishing, and gathering which, combined
with variations in habitat, could have some influence on the
forms of residential groups.

Adaptation with respect to natural environments obviously has, as in the case of band society, relevance to de-

---

[3] Useful discussions of specific processes in clan development have been
made by Titiev (1943) and Goldschmidt (1948).

mographic characteristics. But again, as in the case of band society, demography does not tell us which of the basic social structures will occur. A mere glance around the tribal world shows clearly that neither technology, habitat, demography, nor anything related gives a clue. Perhaps, again as in the case of band society, it is in the character of the superorganic environment that we should seek the basic determinants.

The most striking differences in social organization seem to lie in the various social structures. There are, of course, as many differences of this sort as there are tribes, but such a catalog would fail to get to the point; classification is essential. For better or for worse, the same procedure will be followed as in the previous chapter and two basic, highly generalized polar types of social structure will be described. These are (a) tribes with lineal descent groups; and (b) those that are amorphous, that is, composite. Somewhere between these poles lies a structural type that is relatively rare among tribes, formed of descent groups that are non-lineal, or "cognatic," [4] and this, too, will be given brief consideration as a type.

The tribes known to ethnology are so much more numerous than bands that it is not feasible to discuss a large proportion of them in the fashion of the previous chapter. It might be well, however, to list some examples within the dual classification, selected for diversity in habitat, culture area, and technology. These are only examples, not proofs of anything, given so that the reader may have a somewhat more concrete idea of what and who is under discussion.

Lineal tribes include such well-known groups as the Iroquois of the northeastern woodlands of the United States

---

[4] "Nonunilineal" is frequently used for these descent groups. The "uni-" seems redundant, but otherwise the word is acceptable. Murdock (1960) has criticized it, however, and proposes "cognatic." Cognatic will be used here to refer to residential groups and kin sodalities based on a conception of descent that is not lineal but generalized. Composite groups differ from these in the absence of the descent conception.

(horticulturalists); Hopi, Zuni, and Navaho of the south-western deserts of the United States (horticulturalists and pastoralists); Guaraní, Nambicuara, Bororo, and many others in the tropical forests of South America (horticul-turalists); Nuer, and others of the uplands of East Africa (pastoralists); Boloki, Mongo, and neighbors of Central African forests (horticulturalists); Reindeer Tungus, Soyot, Samoyed of Siberia (pastoralists); some Papuans in the in-land forests of Melanesia (horticulturalists); and the Ifaluk of Micronesia (horticulturalists).

Tribes of composite social structure seem to be those that have experienced breakdown, disorganization, depopu-lation, defeat, removal or some such hazards that have re-sulted in a readaptation of a social basis that is not—perhaps cannot be—on a basis of lineal descent, and mostly not on descent at all. Some modern examples are the Two Moun-tain Iroquois, a refugee tribe near Montreal (horticultural-ists-hunters-fishers); the Eastern Apache in the American Southwest (horticulture-hunting-predation); Rio Grande Pueblos of New Mexico (irrigation horticulture); Coman-che and Cheyenne of the Great Plains (mounted hunters); Carib and Tupían Indians in the Upper Xingú River re-gion of Brazil (horticulturalists); Tenetehara, Tapirapé, Kaingang in Brazil (horticulturalists); the Dobuans, Koita, and Kiwai Papuans in Oceania (all horticulturalists); the Ifugao in the Philippines (irrigation horticulturalists). Many more could be listed, but these are well known and serve sufficiently as diverse examples.

THE LINEAL TRIBE

The basic social characteristics of lineal tribes are rules of unilocal residence and lineal descent reckoning, a social structure of residential groups and sodalities (mainly lin-eages and clans) based on these rules, and status terminol-

ogies which manifest in certain respects the influences of all
of the above.

Rules

Marital residence rules and conceptions of descent may be
either uxorilocal or virilocal and matrilineal or patrilineal.
That virilocal residence and the related conception of patrilineal descent should occur in tribal society is not surprising, considering that virilocality was characteristic of band
society and that the collaborative activities of males in
fighting, hunting, and ceremonial activities remain prominent in tribal society. What is more difficult to explain is
the widespread occurrence of matriliny. Inasmuch as matrilineal descent usually presupposes uxorilocal residence and
the resultant matrilocal kin groups, the essential question
concerns the rise of uxorilocal marital residence rules.

One notes first that uxorilocal-matrilineal tribes are
widely scattered in the primitive world—in parts of North
and South America, Melanesia, Southeast Asia, and Africa
—but also that they are found typically in one kind of
socioeconomic situation: rainfall horticulture with the gar-
dening done by women and with a number of nuclear
families forming a close-knit local kin group, sometimes an
actual residential longhouse.

The suggestion in this situation is that in matrilineal
tribes the significant factor must be the collaborative activities of the women: tending gardens, having common
harvest or food-processing labor and commonly shared food
storage, and in many cases (the Iroquois are a well-known
example), even common cooking for the whole longhouse.
It may be that the cooperation of women makes their continued existence as a group a sufficient reason for uxorilocal
residence, even though hunting and warfare may remain
important collaborative activities of males. With respect to
this latter point, it should be remembered that horticul-

tural tribes are denser than bands so that intermarrying kin groups are no longer scattered distantly; thus brothers and other males who grew up together can continue collaboration as adults even when removed in marriage to different residential groups; and inasmuch as their cooperation is discontinuous and the women's is continuous, the degree of separation of males is not as disruptive as would be the removal of women from their group. Possibly a horticultural tribe is virilocal or uxorilocal depending on the relative strength of these two factors, warfare as opposed to the collaborative raising, processing, storage, and distribution of food.

We rise considerably above mere conjecture in this matter when we consider the unusual opportunity offered the ethnologist Robert Murphy, who was able to investigate a historical shift from virilocal to uxorilocal residence among the Mundurucú Indians of the Brazilian jungle. Mundurucú horticultural labor and the intricate processing of manioc flour were done by females, and the males collaborated in intensive warfare. Under more recent conditions the tribal economy became deeply involved in the sale of manioc flour to Brazilian settlers, while warfare diminished. Over a period of approximately sixty years of this trade the female work group gradually became preeminent as a continuing body and the basis of society changed from a virilocal to a uxorilocal residence pattern (Murphy, 1956). In this one case, at least, we have impressive evidence of the importance of collaborative labor by sex.

Once uxorilocal residence becomes a mode and kin groups develop which are matrilocal, then many other aspects of the social organization become different from those of patrilocal societies. The makeup of the residential groups will obviously be different, as will the nuclear family itself in some respects. As a consequence of these characteristics the status network, and even the very pattern of the egocentric kinship terminology, the most intimate and personal aspects of the society, are often altered in some ways. All of these differences will be discussed in subsequent sections, but they are mentioned now as a reminder of the order of priority of different parts of social organization in the rise of tribal society.

The concept of descent characteristic of unilineal tribes is typically that of common, but not genealogical, descent unless within a very limited range of relatives. This difference will become more apparent in the next chapter where chiefdoms and their striking use of genealogy is discussed; at this point it is necessary only to remark that the conception of descent is closely related to the egalitarian nature of tribal society. In such a society there is no main line of descent predominating over subsidiary lines. All members of the lineage or of kin sodalities such as clans are full members and equally related to the ancestral figure.

With respect to orginating functions it would appear that the residence rule is more important than that of descent reckoning. Unilocal residence directly affects the structure of the residential groups—which, in turn, affects the form of descent reckoning. Thus kinds of lineages, for example, do not result from types of descent, but rather the opposite. Descent as a conception, however, does have a very important creative function in the formation of kin sodalities.

Sodalities are formed "on purpose," so to speak, and the creation of a sodality involves giving it a name, a meaning and purpose, and criteria of membership. Thus if residential groups serve in some respects as models for a kin sodality such as a clan, then probably a name, purpose, and mode of affiliation will be based on those that are characteristic of the residential groups.

It could be argued that true descent reckoning above the level of the family itself first comes about when it is used to make lineal kin sodalities—that this is the first occasion to make it explicit as a conception rather than merely implicit in what was simply a unilocal residence group. Thus a probable developmental sequence may well have been: the unilocal mode of marital residence structures the residential kin group; kin sodalities then take their conceptions from the nature of the unilocal kin group. The name, function, and means of affiliation in the kin sodalities cause unilineal descent to crystallize out as an explicit conception which in turn can be applied back to the residential kin group. Thus in time the original patrilocal or matrilocal residential groups become truly patrilineal or matrilineal lineages.

Social Structure

The lineage is the basic residential unit in lineal tribal society. It is, perforce, either patrilineal or matrilineal and it is a common descent group. The affiliation of new members is, of course, either exclusively maternal or paternal, and by birth, but also the whole group has a putative or real common ancestor. Ordinarily in small lineages which have only a shallow genealogical depth of four or five generations, the common ancestor may be remembered as a real person. The lineal nature of the group is preserved by lineage exogamy; hence the actual composition of the group at any given time includes the permanent core of lineally related persons and also their married-in spouses, who are not truly members of the lineage, at least originally.

Often the lineage has a highly corporate character, holding land and perhaps other property in common, settling the grievances of its members, collaborating in labor, sharing and storing food, and so on. It may be so corporate that the whole lineage might live in a single house, a longhouse, with common cooking, a characteristic of the woodland horticulturalists in both North and South America. In all cases, corporateness is a common characteristic of tribal lineages.

Many kinds of things have been called lineages in an-

thropology and here it may be well to repeat that the subject at hand is residential groups. Sometimes nonresidential
sodalities have been called lineages. As remarked earlier,
sodalities may be formed for many purposes and in many
ways. Sometimes a sodality is, however nonlocal, a lineal
descent sodality with lineal affiliation which has the purpose
of transmitting some kind of property, ritual knowledge, or
whatever, and with a further function (latent or sometimes
manifest) of making more solidary social relations among
different residential lineages. Thus patrilineal lineages
might recognize certain kinds of property, or ritual rights,
or recipes which should pertain to a female descent line
and be inherited maternally, and this situation would at
the same time help retain or strengthen the feeling of kinship between certain persons of the different local lineages.

Sometimes lineages exist in a sort of residual sense. That
is to say, recognition of membership remains although the
lineage's corporate functions have been replaced by some
other body, as when disruptive changes have broken up the
common property rights. Most frequently some kind of
group has formed for whatever expedient reasons—like the
composite local group at the band level—and the original
lineage is left as a scattered "survival" or perhaps only a
memory. Unless it is made into a sodality, however, it can
only last as long as the memories of the particular persons
who compose it.

At this point it is relevant to mention a few of the differences in internal makeup of residential lineages which are
related to the differences between matrilineal and patrilineal descent and associated residence customs. Both kinds
of lineages have the same kinds of problems and corporate
functions. However, the solutions are somewhat different,
inasmuch as the status position of men and women in the
lineage is altered while their basic roles in society are to a
large extent not interchangeable—and this, of course, may
bring up new kinds of subsidiary problems.

One of the most striking of the functional adjustments results from the fact that in both matrilineal and patrilineal groups "husbandness" and familial authority remain male roles even though males reside in wife's lineage in uxorilocal-matrilineal societies rather than in their own. In such societies the problem is met in various ways. In some, the wife's brother takes over many of the authoritarian roles simply because he is the closest male relative who is actually a member of the lineage. There are various other alternatives, but in all cases the nuclear family (particularly the position of husband, or father from the point of view of the children) is very different from the authoritarian, patriarchal setup in patrilineal societies.

A matrilineage reacts on the nuclear family in other striking ways. As implied above, the continuity of the lineage with respect to its corporate functions causes the social bonds between mother and daughter and brother and sister to become stronger than in patrilineal societies at the same time that those between the husband and wife are weaker. Thus a matrilineage may be a more solidary unit in proportion to the weakness of the conjugal bond, whereas in patrilineal societies the stronger conjugal relation is at the same time a frequent source of disunity or contention within the lineage. Another aspect of this situation is that affinal relations in patrilineal and patrilocal societies are clear-cut and ordered, because displaced women are the bond and they are of less political significance than males. Matrilineal societies, on the other hand, frequently have conflicts over authority and position because the male is not "home," so to speak, to exert his authority in his lineage, and if he intervenes in affairs where he does live he is "out of line"—that is, out of his lineage—and should play a more demure role.

Sodalities in lineal tribes are, as remarked earlier, normally based on the conception of lineal descent. Clans are by far the most common, with the other, the so-called segmentary lineage, much more restricted in its distribution.

Clans are simple enough. The members are related by lineal descent to a common ancestor. Because they are not local such things as name, insignia, sometimes dress and particular ceremonial labors are prominent. The ceremonial functions are often so frequent and so important in some societies that these have sometimes been interpreted as the primary function or purpose of clans. But it seems more probable that the ceremonial labors originally came about to maintain the clan rather than the clan to maintain the ceremonies, however important the ceremonies might seem to be eventually.

The ultimate functions of clans vary greatly. In some societies they are landholding, in others ceremonial only, and in others they operate only in the context of war and peacemaking. Yet in all some legal-like corporateness with respect to defense of members occurs. Primarily a clan acts to preserve peaceful relations among its members; it thus has some effect on the relations of residential groups to each other, and acts to adjudicate or end disputes and punish wrongs in relations between members of different clans.

The segmentary lineage system resembles clanship in that it is based on notions of kinship and descent. It is different from clanship, however, in that kinship and descent are more fully conceptualized as genealogy, and the lineages maintain a set of varying relations to each other with respect to putative genealogical distance. The whole tribe seems to have a more organized relationship of its parts, a better integration.

One can think of the relationship of the parts, the association of independent local lineages, in terms of probable origin. When a growing lineal (or unilocal) kin group fissions into two segments the people may continue to conceive of themselves as still something of a kin group, a higher-order lineage composed of two lower-order lineages, with the (putative or actual) common ancestor remembered by both lineages. There would ordinarily be enough of a residential factor left so that the single sodality-like concept of common ancestry remains enough to signify relationship. As the process of growth and segmentation continues, however, the residential factor decreases in significance with respect to the earlier and is greater with respect to the more recently subdivided. To the extent that any common purposes continue for the more distantly related, then common membership approaches more and more that of a sodality and less and less that of a residential group.

It may be an important element in the development of a conception of genealogy that genealogical distance, at least in this case, corresponds to distance in both time and space. At any rate, the scheme of the tribe eventually becomes quasi-genealogical with respect to the relations of the local lineages to each other. The whole tribe—perhaps thousands of people—is a system of the more closely related lineages allied as segments of a conceptualized higher-order lineage, which in turn is allied with others of that order into a still larger, more dispersed lineage of still higher, more abstract, order. This system is not one of rank-order, a hierarchy in power or prestige. It is rather a progression from concrete residential groups to more abstract sodality-like relationships among them, as the geographic distance corresponds to genealogical distance.

The common purpose, the manifest function, of these sodalities appears to be political in the sense that offense-defense alliances are what the relationships are used for. The close kinship of adjacent residential lineages makes it possible for them to combine readily against outsiders. To hold sodality-like connections with more distant lineages is to bring them into the alliance more easily. This also, of course, has the reciprocal effect of helping to secure peace within the area.

The political functions of the segmentary lineage system suggest the specific adaptive situations which operate to bring it about, given the ingredients of unilocal residential groups in an expanding situation. The system seems quite clearly to hinge on the use of kinship conceptions to forge (or keep) alliances, to create solidarity, to take the place of the residential factor as fissioning takes place under competition. The situation involves territorial expansion along with population expansion, of course, and the expansion is *against* somebody. This can be thought of as two kinds of movements; within the territory nuclear lineages expand outward against peripheral lineages; the latter, in turn are pushing, or being pushed, against alien tribes. Such a continuing situation is documented for one of the best-known examples of the segmentary lineage system, the Tiv of Nigeria. The build-up of internal pressure forces the peripheral lineages into a conflict with foreign tribes. Then, as battle is joined against complete aliens, the advanced lineages can muster support from behind them. It seems apparent that this more solidary kind of tribe has a great advantage over nonsegmentary tribes because they can muster larger forces.[5]

Before we leave the subject of sodalities made on the basis of descent it should be mentioned again that sometimes a tribe will have certain kinds of sodalities with paternal affiliation and others with maternal affiliation; sometimes, too, these sodalities may be organized on the basis of patrilineal descent and at other times on the basis of matrilineal descent. These have been called double-descent systems. This is a rather inappropriate designation, however, for it suggests that the whole society is characterized by these two conceptions simultaneously when actually the society is distinctive only in that two kinds of sodalities

---

[5] Discussions of the segmentary lineage may be found in Evans-Pritchard (1940), P. Bohannon (1958), Sahlins (1961, 1968).

with different purposes coexist—that is, there are two kinds of things, not a double thing or combination or system.[6]

At this point, and in this chapter, we must restrict the discussion to tribal society and to sodalities. It is obvious that a tribe can easily use the conception of matrilineal descent for one kind of sodality and patrilineal descent for another, as well as other means of definition. The tribe can also use either maternal or paternal modes of ascribing affiliation and inheritance or succession. But it is a very different matter when local residential groups are being considered. There is absolutely no way that descent as a recognized, conceptualized criterion of the group's composition —or for that matter even of affiliation in a social body— can be double in a residential kin group. It might be bilateral (that is, cognatic or nonlineal) in the sense that any relatives, reckoned by whatever relationship, might belong, but this is merely *general* relationship, not conceptions of two distinct lineal descent lines. A person's own *affiliation,* from his own point of view, might be through a variety of means, but descent as a characteristic of the group must be

---

[6] There has been contradictory usage of the concept of double descent. Frequently it refers to the apparent reckoning of membership or affiliation (not descent) in any kind of social entity—a residential group, sodality, or even status position. Thus some Australian bands are said to be double-descent groups because, for example, a person may reside in his father's area because of virilocal residence (miscalled patrilineal descent), yet recognize some kind of affiliation with his mother's group or moiety (miscalled matrilineal descent), or sometimes inherit certain magical items from her (also miscalled matrilineal descent). Further, the sociocentric status classification (the "section system") itself has been interpreted as caused by double descent, the intersection of patrilocal residence groups with matrilineal moieties (see Murdock, 1949, pp. 50–56).

From the point of view taken here, this interpretation is all wrong. First, nothing in the above is a matter of true *descent* reckoning at all—the anthropologist, not the Australians, is reckoning the descent. Secondly, the sections in Australia are status classifications and not kin groups or social groups of any kind. (Murdock [p. 51] calls them "bilinear kin groups.") This particular matter has been argued at some length elsewhere (Service, 1960a).

either lineal or cognatic. An endogamous community, or one with neither virilocal or uxorilocal modes of marital residence, for example, can be simply a collection of relatives. An anthropologist can, with his paper and pencil, separate people related patrilineally and matrilineally, but to the people involved neither lineal conception is even the basis of affiliation, much less the definition of the descent group; they merely cite their closest relatives in terms of bilateral descent. This could be called "ambiguous affiliation" perhaps, but surely not double descent. These relationships will be discussed more fully in our later discussion of cognatic and composite tribes.

Goody, in a summary article on this subject (1961, p. 8), restricts the use of the double-descent concept to descent groups, which for our present purpose results in some ambiguity in that it does not distinguish between residential groups and sodalities. It seems possible, however, that his conception of descent group could include a sodality: "[it is] . . . an *institutionalized* social group, *recognized by the presence of a technical term* or a distinctive *name,* which is organized on the basis of unilineal consanguinity, actual or supposed. Double-descent systems are those in which a person belongs to a pair of such groups, one based on the patrilineal, the other on the matrilineal, mode of reckoning" (my emphases). Thus it appears that an *individual* may have double descent (or better, "dual membership") when he belongs to two differently constituted groups or sodalities. However, to call a society, or even a part of it such as a group, a double-descent *system* is the often encountered solecism, the confusion of an individual's place in a system with the society itself. There is no such thing as a double-descent society or group; there are only societies which involve individuals in varying social contexts. And there is nothing surprising about the fact that tribal societies contain different kinds of sodalities, defined differently and with different criteria for membership; they may be rare in band society, but they are commonplace at the tribal level and in archaic states and urban societies are multifarious.

Statuses

As tribal social structure is a general advance in complexity over that of band society, so we may expect more kinds and diversification of status terminology and new emphases in tribal society.

The most significant new emphasis in the status terms of tribal society is the increase in the number and importance of sociocentric terms over egocentric terms. The greater complexity of tribal society over band society means that there are more kinds of residential groups, more kinds of sodalities, and more kinds of categories and classes of persons—thus, more kinds of social standings and more differing social contexts in which the standings are operative. Of all of these sociocentric statuses perhaps the most noteworthy are those that refer to groups and sodalities; in some kinds of social intercourse a person is identified by the name or titles referring to his membership in these.

To put the matter another way, there are more different kinds of social persons in tribal society than in bands. And, of course, there is a much larger population and greater density. Egocentric relationships continue, but a greater number of social contexts exist in tribal society which include many persons who are simply not familiar enough to each other for egocentric status terms to be used and the actual social structure of the tribe becomes increasingly the referent of social standings.

It is noteworthy that many of the sociocentric status terms in tribal society are derived from kinship criteria. Thus the terminology is still kinship terminology in the sense that it is familistic, even though it be sociocentric. This reflects the fact that a tribe is more than a small interacting number of close kinsmen among whom egocentric terminology would be appropriate. Yet it is still primarily a society organized in terms of kinlike criteria, though not entirely (a soldier society or ritual-clown society is not necessarily familistic).

Although there is a relative increase in sociocentric status terminology at the tribal level, most of the forms of egocentric terminology that were encountered at the band level continue to exist among tribes, and for the same general reasons. For example, the bifurcate-merging type of egocentric terminology, in which cross and parallel relatives are distinguished, with parallel relatives undistinguished from lineal relatives, is still characteristic of many lineal tribes. It will be recalled that this terminological pattern is a natural result of reciprocal exogamy and unilocal marital residence. Among tribes having lineages, these conditions still obtain—even though the people are more numerous—and the bifurcate-merging terminology thus may be still appropriate. Moreover, clan organization extends the range of this kind of terminology. People of the same sex of the same generation within the clan, inasmuch as they are believed to be descendant in the paternal or maternal line from a common ancestor, may have a common status. Those of the parents' generation within the clan, correspondingly, are of a common status, separated only by sex. Those of the other clan, the group into which one marries, are generalized cross-cousins if of Ego's generation, undifferentiated terminologically as a group but distinguished from those of Ego's own clan. Their parents are accordingly generalized cross-uncles and cross-aunts.

In some cases where lineages and clans are strongly corporate, the widespread bifurcate-merging terminology undergoes further specific change. Clan and/or lineage membership may become such an important aspect of social interaction that the status of a person of Ego's affinal group —his father's clan or lineage in a matrilineal society, the mother's in a patrilineal society—becomes more importantly a matter of group membership than of the more individualized, more specific, egocentric relationship. Thus the bifurcate-merging type of egocentric nomenclature remains characteristic of Ego's social relationship to members of his own clan and lineage, with whom he has close and frequent interaction, but in dealings with members of the affinal lineage or clan the terminology normally used is sociocentric, meaning something like "male (female) of the such-and-such clan (or lineage)." Generic names have been given this overriding of the egocentric terminology by a sociocentric term in situations like the above: "Crow system" when the affinal group is father's (that is, a matrilineal society) and "Omaha system" when it is mother's (a patrilineal society).

There is nothing very surprising about the replacement of one kind of terminology by another in certain social contexts. In our own society sons have been heard to refer to their own father as "The Doctor" or uncles and nephews call each other "brother" at a lodge meeting or a person may call his brother "Mr. President." At the band level a person belongs to only a few statuses at any one time and because of close personal associations most of the statuses are egocentric. As society becomes larger and more complex a person simultaneously holds more and more statuses and there are more and more different kinds of contexts of interpersonal relations so that the term used the most frequently is often a sociocentric term; it is also, ultimately, more often a nonfamilistic term, as social relations become more multifarious, distant, and pertain to group more than to personal relations.

COGNATIC AND COMPOSITE TRIBES

The social structure of cognatic and composite tribes differs (obviously, from the names given them) from lineal tribes in the absence of lineality in residential groups and (usually) in sodalities. A nonlineal, or cognatic, group is composed simply of descendants traced through either or both mother's and father's relatives. The residential group normally would not include all of the descendants, of course, but may be a core of closely linked relatives.

Rules

The descent reckoning is thus general and unspecific. Marital residence is, of course, an unspecific counterpart of the relatively amorphous structure of the group—that is, it is merely expedient. Even if the residence groups are exogamous (and they may or may not be) the newly marrieds might live with whatever group of relatives they find most receptive.

An important characteristic of both cognatic and composite groups is suggested by this lack of specificity in marital residence modes. Affiliation is expedient and not fixed by birth, whereas one is born into a lineage and membership is for life. This relative openness means that the groups can alter their size. This latter characteristic makes for residential groups which might have adaptive advantages in some circumstances.

Social Structure

In thinking about the possible origins of cognatic residential groups in terms of adaptation it may again be helpful to separate environment into the two variable aspects, the natural and the superorganic.

Any groups whose membership is fixed by birth, such as lineages, will fluctuate differentially in size; in time some may become quite large and must fission and spread while others remain stable or decline. If an area is open and uncontested, growing lineages may simply split and the lineal structure of the resulting segments be preserved. If the area is contested by others, the same thing can happen if the spreading groups are successful in competing against them. On the other hand, if the tribal domain is bounded by either stronger enemies or natural barriers, as on a small island, growing residential groups must either fight each other or adjust their size to the territorial domain they already hold. The simplest way to make this adjustment is to allow members of residential groups to change their affiliation to smaller groups. This, of course, would ordinarily be done on the occasion of marriage, allowing marital residence to become economically and socially expedient rather than according to a consistently unilocal pattern.

Some reasons for thinking that the above circumstances could have had an influence on the origin of cognatic groups can be found in the actual geographic distribution of the two kinds of tribes. The tribal societies with strong corporate lineages seem to be typically horticulturalists and pastoralists who do in fact have either the free area or the fighting ability to alter the amounts of territory controlled and thus maintain the lineality of fissioning groups. On the other hand, there are many small islands in the Pacific where land cannot be expanded and where, appropriately for this theory, cognatic groups exist along with the absence of a unilocal residence mode. On the tiny Melanesian Island of Dobu, for example, a de jure lineage-like organization has been maintained as a sort of sodality while the residence rule was compromised expediently. Apparently residential lineages become disrupted in this way, with some lineality maintained only on a nonlocal basis. Similar disturbances caused by restricted lands occurred in the Gilbert Islands and other islands in Micronesia.[7]

Sometimes a kind of compromise has been made which results in a residential group that is a mixture of lineal

---

[7] See Goodenough (1955) for the original theory of nonunilineal descent groups in relation to bounded territories.

and cognatic principles. It has a core of permanent inhabitants of a region who are related lineally, but other
kinds of relatives join this nucleus for long periods as resources are needed by them or leave when resources are
scarce. Thus some of the people have unilocal residence rules
and others reside where the situation permits, depending
on the amount of imbalance between population and resources in any given locality. The permanent core would
seem to have certain powers or rights greater than the impermanent families, or else such powers or rights would
soon accrue to them under the circumstances. Fried (1957,
p. 22) suggests that such situations are related to the possible genesis of social stratification.

Although open as opposed to closed territory could be
related to the presence of lineal as opposed to cognatic
residential groups in tribal society, we have so far ignored
a rather different aspect of the superorganic environment,
the impact of civilization. This impact has various features
and significances as well as varying strength. We may suppose that its influence on the formation of cognatic structures is partial and not drastic. There would seem to be a
number of ways by which the law and order imposed by
colonial powers, and in some cases by a reservation system,
could have the effect of restricting or even reducing the territories controlled by the tribal kin groups without otherwise disturbing the tribe.

Composite tribes, on the other hand, are those whose
breakdown and subsequent readaptation was greater because of a stronger influence of civilization. One salient consequence of civilization on a great many tribes has been
depopulation through foreign disease, most usually carried
by Europeans; another is disturbance of the resource base
by such things as economic exploitation and alienation of
native lands or outright removal; still another, but frequently overemphasized in studies of changes in social or-

ganization, is acculturation—direct borrowing of traits from the invaders. There are, of course, other consequences which could be listed, but at this point we need not get too involved in this complex situation; for present purposes it is sufficient to establish that a great many tribal peoples have been drastically altered—sometimes nearly destroyed—by civilization, and that a very common result has been that those who survived with some tribal identity typically have composite groups instead of lineal descent groups.

Not enough historical research has been done to establish the above argument firmly as a generalization, but it seems increasingly compelling when one considers recent ethnographic studies of some particular regions. Both Eggan (1937) and Spoehr (1947) are concerned with groups in the southeastern United States. These groups are considered chiefdoms in this book, hence more relevant to our next chapter. They are mentioned now as being suggestive of the sorts of changes that can as well, or even more easily, happen to tribal society. Wagley (1940) has documented the social results of depopulation for one tribal society in South America, the Tapirapé, and Eggan (1950, pp. 313–321) has suggested that the relative absence of lineality, the great incidence of bilateral kinship and the rise of what are here called sodalities in the Eastern Pueblos of the Rio Grande Valley as opposed to the lineality of the Western Pueblos are significantly associated with greater Spanish influence in the former.

Dole (1957, pp. 290–361) has made a convenient summary of the differences between what she calls "formal" and "informal," or fluid, kin groups in three widely separated world areas: the North American Plains, Oceania, and tropical South America. Bands, tribes, and chiefdoms are all included in her summary. She found a strong association between generational kinship terminology and disruption due to European contact in all three areas and—more relevantly for the present point—a similarly strong association between disruption and subsequent informal (composite) residential groups.[8]

Thus it seems possible and even probable, though not proved, that corporate lineages are the normal aboriginal form of tribal residential groups and that the composite groups correspond to the breakup of tribal organization after the impact of modern civilization. This is not to say that tribes were not sometimes similarly disorganized by other and earlier catastrophes and environmental circumstances of a different sort; but that disruption must have been only at some times and in only some places, whereas the influences of modern civilization on tribes have become permanent and nearly world-wide.

Sodalities in cognatic and composite tribes are sometimes formed on the basis of descent and kinship, but ordinarily not on conceptions of lineality. In cognatic tribes the counterpart of the clan is the kindred, a nonlocal sodality of relatives traced nonlineally. Sometimes there are sodalities which resemble kinship sodalities in that affiliation is by kin relationship (from father to son, or mother's brother to son, or whatever), but the sodality itself will not be constituted primarily of certain kinds of kinsmen, nor defined as such. Sodalities might be organized for a variety of special purposes, yet all will have latent integrating functions to the extent that they cross-cut residential groups.

Some sodalities have expressly political purposes. The Plains Indian Age-Grade, Military, or Soldier Societies can quickly organize for offense or defense, and some of them have as a primary purpose the control of individuals in times of great communal hunts or tribal ceremonies. In

---

[8] Since the present book was written an article by R. B. Lane (1961) has appeared which documents the change from lineal descent groups (and associated Crow terminology) to "amorphous" (composite) groups with generational terminology among the Banks Islanders and the Barabet region of the New Hebrides. In both cases the cause was clearly rapid and drastic depopulation due to introduced diseases.

Melanesia it is very common that secret men's societies have as the primary manifest function the performance of religious rites. Yet it could be held that the rites and feasts they sponsor are really only appurtenances of the sodality, that they help keep the sodality solidary, whereas political control, warfare, and the creation of leadership in the society are the primary functions, whether manifest to some extent or latent.

It is possible that non-kin sodalities are in some sense alternatives to kinship sodalities in tribal organization. Such a judgment not only conforms to the present notions of the functions of sodalities but also seems to have some basis in ethnographic fact. Most prominent of the examples are the buffalo-hunting tribes of the American Great Plains. The offense-defense problem in the Plains was a constant feature of life and political consolidation was therefore of great importance. All of the Plains tribes lacked true lineal residential groups, although some had had them, as well as clans, before they became equestrian in the Plains. It would seem also that the tribes were often formed by amalgamation rather than internal growth. Appropriately, the Plains tribes had a marked efflorescence of clubs, societies, and age-graded associations. This judgment does not mean that the presence of clans, segmentary lineages, or kindreds *precludes* the rise of non-kin sodalities, for they should be expected to come about in proportion to the need for them; it is merely a way of saying that the need for non-kin sodalities is greater if there are no kin sodalities, or if the kin sodalities are too weak.[9]

Status Terminology

Inasmuch as cognatic and composite tribes are less formal, or less structured, than lineal tribes with respect to their

---

[9] S. N. Eisenstadt has reasoned similarly about Plains Indian age-grade groupings (1954, p. 7).

kin groups it might be expected that they would exhibit more kinds of nonfamilistic status positions. But this is pure conjecture.

As mentioned with respect to lineal tribes, sociocentric kin terminology is more frequent at the tribal level than at the band level. I have no idea, however, whether there might be more or less of it among cognatic and composite as opposed to lineal tribes.

Of egocentric kin terminologies the so-called Hawaiian or generational terminology is by far the most usually associated with cognatic and composite tribes. Relatives are distinguished by generation only, which is to say that affinal (or cross-parallel) distinctions are not made, nor is there any influence of lineage or lineality as in the Crow-Omaha variations on bifurcate-merging terminology. It should be remarked that generational terminology is not limited to the tribal level, but can occur at any level when residential kin groups are amorphous or unimportant for whatever reason. Among tribes it would appear that the usual causes of this are depopulation, disruption, dislocation, and so on which destroy the lineal social structure and the unilocal residence mode. But this is not always the cause at higher levels; we shall see that among chiefdoms, for example, egocentric kinship distinctions of the bifurcate-merging sort can become subordinated and relatively nonfunctional in status usage as rank and stratification become more important as statuses in interpersonal conduct.

Now, lest the description of status terminology of tribes seem oversimple to an ethnologically sophisticated reader, it should be noted that many tribes combine different types of terminology. A generational kind might be used in address and an older, residual type still be used in reference. Further, in any given tribe cousin terminology may be generational and parental terminology may be bifurcate-merging. The types outlined so far are not, as patterns of terminology, themselves fully systemic: that is, different parts of the terminology and, particularly, different means of classifying relatives of given generations, can vary independently. A tribe that has gone through a succession of social changes in the relatively recent past may combine the influence of previous social groupings with some late changes in its kinship terminology. It is not simply that the terminology as a whole reflects a prior marriage mode, lineality, or such, but that some part—say, cousin terminology—reflects a present form, whereas another part is related to an earlier one. Statements such as "Crow terminology is associated with corporate matrilineal organization," must carry the proviso that other things are equal, or more precisely, that social organization has been stable over a relatively long period. If the tribe has gone through a succession of adaptive changes in the recent past, as many tribes have, such a rule should not be expected to hold.

THE TRIBAL LEVEL OF SOCIOCULTURAL INTEGRATION

The tribal level as a cultural type is obviously more complex than the band level, with new forms of integration and with greater specific diversification. Yet a tribe is like a band society in some important characteristics which set off both of them from higher levels: they are largely familistic cultures; they are egalitarian; in neither one has differentiation of structure been carried to the point where they have separated bodies of political control, economic specialization (other than the universal age-sex differentiation), or even true religious professionalization (religious specialists exist in both but they are not professionalized groups like priesthoods).

Tribes, like bands, are what Durkheim (1933) called "segmental organizations," meaning that the basic residential units of the society are like each other, largely self-sufficient economically with each enjoying a great deal of autonomy. But tribes tend toward disunity, being larger than bands, and have had to erect more integrating sodalities than have bands.

It could be argued that the development of tribes is actually hindered or restricted to a certain level just because the residential units have similar functions, are generally equivalent in size and organization, and are equal in social status and power. If the general evolution of society consists, as some have said, of not only a multiplication of groups but also of an increase in specialization into economic and political parts, ritual units, and the like, then tribes have advanced over bands only in the sense of multiplication and integration of parts. This is why the present book chooses as the discriminating criterion of stages the *form of integration*. At each level the integration of parts is carried out differently.

But now we should note that Durkheim's idea of segmental organization has as its opposite another kind which he called organic. Specialization and the consequent mutual dependence of *unlike* parts, as implied in the term "organic," do obviously have great integrating effect. Hence the "mechanical" feature of tribes and bands is not so much a cause of solidarity; it is merely the absence of organic solidarity. As we shall see, the biggest difference between bands and tribes, on the one hand, and chiefdoms and all higher levels on the other lies in the relative importance of organic interdependence of parts. It is now, at the point of moving to the level of chiefdoms, that our basic criterion of stages, which is consistently directed to the form of integration, finds organic solidarity—or specialization of parts —relevant because it is the form of integration characteristic of chiefdoms.

5

The Social Organization of Chiefdoms

A chiefdom occupies a level of social integration which transcends tribal society in two important respects. First, a chiefdom is usually a denser society than is a tribe, a gain made possible by greater productivity. But second, and more indicative of the evolutionary stage, the society is also more complex and more organized, being particularly distinguished from tribes by the presence of centers which coordinate economic, social, and religious activities. The term "chiefdom" seems more appropriate than the several alternatives because it focuses attention on the rise of this sociopolitical innovation. It has been used by Oberg (1955), and after him by Steward and Faron (1959), to designate a type of South American Indian society. The present usage somewhat simplifies this regional type and extends it to designate a stage in general cultural evolution.

The increased productivity and greater population density of chiefdoms are not necessarily due to any particular technological development, although in some instances it is apparent that such development did take place. More frequently, and in all cases importantly, the rise of chiefdoms seems to have been related to a total environmental situation which was selective for specialization in production and redistribution of produce from a controlling center. The resulting organic basis of social integration made possible a more integrated society, and the increased efficiency in production and distribution made possible a denser society.

Specialization in production and redistribution of produce occur sporadically and ephemerally in both bands and tribes. The great change at the chiefdom level is that specialization and redistribution are no longer merely adjunctive to a few particular endeavors, but continuously characterize a large part of the activity of the society. Chiefdoms are *redistributional societies* with a permanent central agency of coordination. Thus the central agency comes to have not only an economic role—however basic this factor in the origin of this type of society—but also serves additional functions which are social, political, and religious.[1] Once it is in existence it can, in other words, act to foster and preserve the integration of the society for the sake of integration alone.

THE RISE OF CHIEFDOMS

Chiefdoms are found today in many parts of the world: in North and South America, Africa, Southeast Asia, Inner Asia, and some of the Pacific Islands. In the archaeological record they are probably at least as widely represented, particularly in the strata underlying the archaic civilizations of Peru and Middle America, the eastern Mediterranean, India, and China. But one must say "probably" in these cases because, as mentioned above, chiefdoms are not always demarked by a particular technological innovation which would set them off from tribes and states, but are charac-

---

[1] For a discussion of redistribution in relation to social and political organization in Polynesia see Sahlins (1958); of interest with respect to Northwest Coast Indians are Drucker (1939) and Suttles (1960).

terized by their form of organization, most of which is not revealed in archaeological deposits; they can only be inferred or conjectured.[2]

No one has observed the actual origin of a chiefdom. Nevertheless, we do have good ethnological information on chiefdoms in various degrees of development and it is not particularly difficult to imagine the conditions which would be selective for the rise of a redistributional society. Clearly, redistribution is a consequence of specialization and the related needs for its coordination and for the allocation of products.

There are two distinct and separable kinds of specialization which could lead to redistribution. They frequently coexist in the same society, but it seems probable that one or the other alone would be sufficient to catalyze the transformation of society. One (probably the more frequent) is the regional specialization of different local residential units; the other is the pooling of individual skills in large-scale cooperative productive endeavors.

A great many of the ethnologically known chiefdoms exist in habitats that consist of several zones differentiated by climate, soil, rainfall, and natural products. (See the later breakdown of the distribution of well-known chiefdoms.) Frequently these habitats are mountainous, so that differences in altitude, sunny and shady slopes, alluvial valleys, forests and open lands, rainfall differences and the like promote a local differentiation in the kinds of crops grown as well as in the distribution of natural products like wood, fish, game, fruit, nuts, roots, and so on. Without agriculture, people would take advantage of that variation by moving themselves around with respect to the products. With agriculture and permanent settlements, the local specialization is most

---

[2] Several American archaeologists have recently inferred the ranks and strata of chiefdoms and states convincingly from aspects of archaeological remains. See, as good examples, MacNeish (1964), Adams (1966), Binford and Binford (1968), and Sanders and Price (1968).

advantageous to the inhabitants when the products are moved.

Reciprocal exchanges of goods between inhabitants of different specialized zones seem to have taken place to some extent in both bands and tribes. Our concern here is with the *amount* of exchange and its degree of economic and social significance which could transform a society to the chiefdom level. Two variables could affect this amount and significance: (a) The degree of sedentariness; the more sedentary the residential groups the more likely that goods rather than people will be moved. (b) The actual degree of regional differentiation, for the more distinct the zones the more necessary, or at least the more useful, are exchanges among them. Most chiefdoms seem to have risen where important regional exchange and a consequent increase in local specialization came about because differentiation in habitat was combined with considerable sedentariness.

Pastoral chiefdoms, of course, are not sedentary, but the amount of regional exchange is proportionately greater because no pastoralists are near to self-sufficiency. They are all economic "part-societies" in symbiosis with sedentary agricultural societies which have vegetables, grains, and craft goods for exchange (or to be plundered sometimes). In fact, it would seem that the economic symbiosis must have been well-established *before* pastoralist chiefdoms could become so specialized as herders.

Primitive reciprocal exchanges that are between societies are never simply matters of individual initiative, but are always of public, or group, interest. This requires an organization of production to create a surplus for the exchange and reciprocally, that which is received in exchange must be redistributed to the people. Organization—which implies some form of leadership—thus is involved in both the producing and receiving aspect of the exchange.

There could have been considerable variation in the relative importance of the producing, as opposed to the receiving, end of the exchange. Some forms of production, by the nature of the technology and habitat, necessitate more specialization, coordination, and direction than others. For example, in order to fully exploit the fantastic salmon runs of the Northwest Coast, an all-out community effort was necessary, with a complex division of labor and subsequent organized allocation of the catch among the individual subgroups. Large-scale herding, whaling, coordinated game drives, and the like also must involve specialization of roles and central direction.

The relation of productivity to redistribution can thus be seen in two aspects. On the one hand, the higher the productivity the more of a surplus can be produced for exchange, which in turn stimulates the tendency toward redistribution from a central authority. On the other hand, as indicated above, certain productive enterprises by their own nature result in some specialization and redistribution. But in either emphasis, specialization and central direction must be clearly advantageous in increasing production.

The above emphasis on regional exchange is again a way of stressing the significance of the superorganic aspect of the environment as part of the total adaptive situation. (See Lesser, 1961, pp. 45–46 for a strong argument for the importance of regional exchanges.) But so far the character of the competitive circumstances has not been discussed sufficiently. As Carneiro has shown (in Wilbert, 1961, pp. 47–67), very often a tribal economy has considerable potentiality for improved production but does not institute it unless some external force such as competition or warfare requires it. The case of the Maori of New Zealand is instructive here as an illustration. The Maori originally came from the central region of Polynesia where chiefdoms were highly developed, but when they colonized the huge, open environment of New Zealand they subdivided and scattered. In so doing they reverted to a less centralized and less organized form of society, eventually coming to resemble tribal society more than their original chiefdom form.

It may also be presumed that the higher the productivity of a society and the more *organized* the production and redistribution, the more of an advantage such a society will have in competitive circumstances. Organization and specialization in economy under some form of leadership could carry over into other affairs, particularly with respect to warfare. The rise of more permanent leadership would seem to be related at first to redistribution, but eventually to have functions in other kinds of activities.

Whether a particular chiefdom begins in specialization for regional exchange or in circumstances which developed coordination of specialized skills in particular local endeavors, it is plain that either factor tends to foster the development of the other. Once centralized direction begins, in other words, it is so advantageous that it extends itself into new areas. Thus we see that a fully developed chiefdom is likely to have both regional specialization *and* individual division of labor tied into the redistribution. Needless to say, a sudden spurt in the relative size of a chiefdom over a tribe is likely, as is improvement in the quality of certain of the products.

Some of the products of primitive skills are in their nature capable of great improvement under specialization. Pottery- and basketmaking, weaving, carpentry and wood carving, for example, were practiced in tribal society only by semispecialists at best. In a chiefdom superior workers can be subsidized. This typically seems to result in the specialization of a family line; the job becomes hereditary and the work becomes increasingly skilled. One of the most striking things about the evolution of culture is the rapid improvement in the products of craft specialization at the point of the rise of chiefdoms.

Specialized crafts are sometimes subsidized at the redistributional center. This subsidization occurs because food and other necessities are being received by the chief at regular intervals; some are redistributed, some are stored for special purposes, such as war or a forthcoming festival or possible famine. Having control of the magazine, the chief can support the specialists.

The rise of subsidized specialists raises the productive level of the society, but here we face the fact also that some specialties may be of no use to the society at all in the economic sense. A chief can support more wives, private shamans, entertainers for his own delectation, weavers and potters who produce only for his household, and so on. When chieftainship becomes a permanent *office* in the structure of society social inequality becomes characteristic of the society, followed finally by inequality in consumption.

Who is the redistributor? This is obviously a position of responsibility and judgment. Leaders can exist for special purposes at any level of society and tend to rise in any cooperative program of action. The redistributor in the beginning would be likely to be that person who is ascendant in community service in the particular endeavor—probably the man who contributes the most to it. At any rate, when the person as redistributor is in that position consistently the situation changes. He begins as redistributor because of prestige achieved as a contributor or some other role; finally, he holds a status because he *is* the redistributor. As the system develops and specialization and redistribution become a necessary and integral part of the social and economic scheme, this central office confers very high rank.

The creation of the hereditary office of chief, with its high status for the person who occupies it, naturally carries the possibility of other statuses of high degree. We might think of the beginning of this system as an otherwise egalitarian society with but one exalted social position. But because societies are composed of solidary family units united into larger residential groups, it is natural that a chief's high

status raises the status of every member of his family above
ordinary families, and ultimately that of the families in
his local kin group to some extent. It has been noted in
European history how a new king creates his own nobility
simply by having a family and descendants. Analogously, a
chief necessarily has a "nobility," even though they are only
his own family. In time, he *and* his brothers, his sons and
their sons, and so on, go on proliferating so that the chiefly
lineage becomes very large and has numerous connections of
different kinds with other lineages. Some of the well-known
chiefdoms, such as the Polynesians and some Indians of the
Northwest Coast of North America, arrived at the point
where every member of the society bore some precise hereditary status which could be calculated in terms of nearness to the chiefly line. We shall return to this point later;
here is noted only the fact that a chiefdom differs radically
from a tribe or band not only in economic and political
organization but in the matter of social rank—bands and
tribes are egalitarian, chiefdoms are profoundly inegali-
tarian. But however salient the personal, individual ranking as a social feature of developed chiefdoms, it should be
reemphasized now that this is a *consequence* of the development of a coordinating center, not its cause. It is the
presence of the office of chief that makes a chiefdom.

A further important feature lies in the chief's ability to
plan, organize, and deploy public labor. This can have, in
certain circumstances, tremendous economic consequences
for a society. Many chiefdoms in mountainous terrains have
terraced slopes to increase the agricultural area. More significant are those which have terraced land and irrigation
works. These are fairly common among the New World and
Polynesian chiefdoms, but the works are always rather limited in extent because they are confined to a single stream
valley. The irrigation works of chiefdoms are limited for
another important reason, too. In areas such as coastal Peru,
the Valley of Mexico (actually a huge basin rather than a

valley), the Tigris-Euphrates and the Indus and Yellow river basins, where the circumstances for water control (irrigation and/or drainage) were not narrowly limited by the terrain, the logic of the situation eventually led to huge interconnected canals. Once this kind of project was well under way, the societies were transformed to a new level—the classical archaic states—thereby obliterating the antecedent chiefdoms after a brief life span.

So far the major characteristics of chiefdoms have been outlined as related to surmises about their origin. But their origin has been considered in terms of what might be called a pristine condition of isolation from other chiefdoms. Yet once chiefdoms and the later primitive states are in existence new chiefdoms can arise as a result of their influence, as "secondary" chiefdoms. Their origin must be viewed, therefore, as adaptation not only to the natural environment but to the superorganic surroundings of competing chiefdoms as well.

As usual when we consider adaptation in the superorganic context, warfare merges as a salient and dramatic feature, though by no means the only one. We may, therefore, begin with the influence of warfare on chiefdoms. It is possible that intense competition and frequent warfare among tribes was an important condition for the rise of chiefdoms in the first place, inasmuch as planning and coordination have obvious advantages in war. However that may be, once a chiefdom (even slightly developed) is pitted against mere tribes it will prevail, other things being equal. But "prevailing" may have several consequences. The vanquished may be driven out, exterminated, kept as captives and sacrificial victims, or incorporated as a people within the borders of the chiefdom. This last possibility deserves some attention, for it has implications for development that the others do not.

A redistributional economy has potentiality for expansion —of its internal population or through incorporation of others—that tribes and bands lack. This is particularly true when different localities are specialized, for it is advantageous to the original society to have new contributions, and obviously advantageous to an incorporated group to participate in the redistribution if it is allowed to do so without disability. It is, in fact, clear from the record in some cases and probable in many others that small neighboring societies, or parts of them, often join an adjacent chiefdom quite voluntarily because of the benefits of participation in the total network. Whatever the means, it is plain that unless they are too hindered by geographic barriers, chiefdoms tend to expand by accretion when their neighbors are similar in language and culture.

Any local group, even if only tribally organized, becomes transformed in the process of incorporation into a chiefdom. A chiefdom is in a sense pyramidal or cone-shaped in structure, and the hierarchical nature of the totality becomes reflected in the smaller local organizations. A local kin group becomes a subsidiary and miniature chiefdom; it needs its own chief to collect goods to be passed up the line to the higher chief and to receive in turn those goods to be redistributed to his people. Likewise with the organization of labor: some work of a purely local nature is planned and administered by this subsidiary chief; but he is also required to lend some of his labor force for the larger plan of the society. Similarly, he and his group play subsidiary roles in the wider religious functions, while he remains in charge of the more specifically local ceremonies and other functions. Thus a pyramidal organization, however small, subsidiary and dependent, is created where there was none before.

The expansion of a chiefdom presumably can go on to the point of exceeding its ability to function efficiently and it may then fall into two or more parts. The "rise and fall" of chiefdoms has been such a frequent phenomenon that it seems to be a part of their nature. (There are, of course, always specific precipitating events which are interpreted as "causes" of the fall: quarrels over succession to the chieftainship, a revolt by groups on the periphery, warfare, etc.) At any rate, new smaller chiefdoms are left to compete for their own expansion. The fact that there is frequently a contiguous belt of chiefdoms suggests the possibility that the cycle of expansion by incorporation and subsequent disintegration is a common cause of the origin and spread of many chiefdoms.

It is also possible that just plain warfare between a chiefdom and adjacent tribes could lead tribes to remake themselves politically, copying the salient features of a chiefdom, in order to resist incorporation more successfully. This proposition cannot be exemplified from the ethnographic record, and we lack adequate histories of chiefdoms which might throw light on it, but it has a certain reasonableness.

The Distribution of Chiefdoms

THE AMERICAS. The so-called "Circum-Caribbean" chiefdoms (Steward, 1948) of the Northern Andes, Central America, Venezuelan coast, larger islands of the West Indies, and southeastern United States, in mountainous regions or coastal and riverine habitats of considerable diversification. Horticulture-hunting-fishing technology.

The Northwest Coast of North America, from Northern California to Alaska. Coastal and riverine habitat with great abundance of fish, shellfish, and sea mammals. Complicated and ingenious hunting-fishing technology and storage techniques.

INDONESIA. Indonesia has been governed for so long by foreign empires, and lately by indigenous governments, that it is impossible to do more than guess that there were probably once a number of chiefdoms of the order of the ethnographically described Bontok Igorot and Menangkabau. Intensive horticulture and domestic animals.

ASIA. The steppe nomads such as the Volga Kalmuk, the

Khalkhas, Chahars, and Dagurs of Mongolia, and the Kazak of Turkestan, and also probably the famous Turkic and Mongol "hordes" of nearly a thousand years ago (before the "Empires"). Large-scale pastoralism of a complex of animals.

In Arabia, the larger "sheikhdoms" qualify as chiefdoms, while many of the local bedouin entities are segmentary-lineage (tribal) in character. However, succession by primogeniture, where it occurs, seems to be the result of European political influence (communication from W. D. Schorger).

OCEANIA. Chiefdoms are most typical and most highly developed on the Polynesian and Micronesian high islands, diminishing in size and complexity on progressively smaller islands. In Fiji, Polynesian outliers (such as Tikopia), and a few Melanesian areas such as the Trobriands are low-level or proto-chiefdoms, but the larger Papuan population of New Guinea mostly remains organized as tribes. Coastal and mountainous habitats. Fishing and intensive horticultural technology.

AFRICA. In West Africa it seems clear that such states as Ashanti, Benin, and Dahomey consisted of a series of smaller chiefdoms before the era of the great slave trade and of European domination. Possibly the East African states were preceded by chiefdoms also. This is clearly the case in South Africa. In modern times there are a few simple chiefdoms in the Nuba Hills of the Upper Nile region and in the Congo Basin and Liberia. Horticulture-hunting-fishing technology.

EUROPE. Scottish Highlanders seem to have been organized into chiefdoms until nearly modern times. These groups have been miscalled "clans" as well as "kingdoms." The Germanic tribes at the time of the Roman incursions sound like chiefdoms, and probably a great many others in Europe preceded the later states and empires.

As in the case of bands and tribes, chiefdoms have been

destroyed, diminished, remade, or otherwise profoundly affected by the influence of civilization in their areas. But we cannot create a category of broken-down or reconstituted chiefdoms because once the structure is destroyed it ceases to be a chiefdom; a chiefdom is defined in terms of its peculiar structure.

The influence of foreign civilization on chiefdoms seems to have taken two different directions. Depopulation, defeat, and dislocation, if they are severe enough, reduce the chiefdom to its tribal-like constituent parts or even to the band level or outright extinction. These were consequences most saliently recorded in the history of the Circum-Caribbean chiefdoms after the coming of the Spaniards to the New World (Steward, 1948), and for refuge-area Turkic groups in Central Asia (Krader, 1955, pp. 87–88). On the other hand, chiefdoms may ascend to the level of primitive states with the great increase in competition, and often, with newly acquired weapons. This consequence was strikingly demonstrated in the cases of Tonga, Tahiti, Hawaii, and some of the West African coastal states. In some other areas, such as parts of the North American Northwest Coast, the contact was at first sporadic and largely commercial and the depopulation of such slight degree that the pyramidal organization remained *in situ,* but with great intensification of status rivalry as the society became more open.

RULES

The most distinctive characteristic of chiefdoms as compared to tribes and bands is, as discussed earlier, the pervasive inequality of persons and groups in the society. It begins with the status of chief as he functions in the system of redistribution. Persons are then ranked above others according to their genealogical nearness to him. Concepts involving prescriptions, proscriptions, sumptuary laws, marriage rules and customs, genealogical conceptions, and etiquette in general combine to create and perpetuate this sociopolitical ordering, and in turn have an effect on social structure and status terminology and etiquette behavior.

A charismatic ephemeral leader of the type found in tribes and bands has the functions and attributes that result from his own capabilities. An "office," on the other hand, is a position in a sociopolitical structure that has ascribed functions and conventionalized attributes no matter who occupies it. There may, of course, be some element of charisma in any given chief's activities; the office is filled by an individual person and he may fill it well or poorly or even add attributes that finally become conventional expectations. (Europe had "strong kings" and "weak kings" and some of the former were so successful that the "King" turned into an "Emperor.") However variable it may be, the office remains and subsidiary offices appear under it as a chiefdom develops.

Probably the first rules peculiar to chiefdoms, and those which importantly affect the rest of the society, are those concerned with the creation and perpetuation of the office of Chief. These are regulations which separate the Chief from all others; sanctify or otherwise legitimatize him; codify his rights, privileges, and duties; and prescribe the form of succession. This last is particularly important in making an office of the post, for continuity from generation to generation is implied in the concept. Thus there would seem to be with respect to the office of Chief two distinct kinds of rules: sumptuary rules or taboos which set aside the chiefly persons into a special category; and rules of succession and affiliation to this category, and to the various groups and ranks.

In the previous section were discussed the circumstances which can elevate a person to a regulatory position. Such a position is not yet sociologically *constituted,* however, until rules and sanctions—a sort of quasi-legality—make over

that preeminent position so that it exists independently of
the particular qualities of the person filling it. Sumptuary
regulations and customs have perhaps the most noticeable
effects in creating separate classes of persons. Distinctiveness
in dress and ornamentation seem to be the most visible of
these and probably the simplest, and perhaps the first, that
were instituted. Others may involve food, diversions, ritual
positions, and sometimes even distinctiveness in vocabulary.
Any of these can be phrased as taboos (a frequent practice
in Polynesia) or as prescriptions, but in either case the aim
seems to be the creation of new and permanent kinds of social persons.

Presumably sumptuary rules begin in isolating the chiefly
personage, but as time goes on they become applied to the
proliferating descendants in some degree; eventually, therefore, rules of succession are needed. Succession to hierarchical offices in chiefdoms seems normally to be characterized
by the rule of primogeniture. Primogeniture can also be
thought of as a matter of inheritance, inasmuch as the offices
are typically and ideally hereditary, given an undisturbed,
stable condition. But once in existence primogeniture modi-
fies also the conceptions of descent and affiliation to groups.

The office of Chief is occupied by one man and thus can
be inherited by only one person. This person is the eldest
son, or sister's eldest son in the more rare matrilineal chiefdom. In theory a system of ultimogeniture would do as well,
for it, too, singles out a lone inheritor, but we must reckon
with the apparently natural fact that the eldest son tends
to be the superordinate one in any family unless he is for
some reason obviously inadequate. Ultimogeniture occurs
rarely in the world, but when it does it seems to be because
the position, property, or whatever, carries responsibilities
which are not desired by the older children. In the history
of rural areas in the United States, for example, when small
farming declines in importance and other, more desirable,
urban occupations are open, the elder sons may go away

to the city by preference, leaving the care of the parents and management of the rundown homestead to the youngest son. This is ultimogeniture in the sense that the youngest inherited the position. That it was rejected by the eldest, however, points up the very general social prerogatives that in any society seem to fall to him. In a stable society the high-ranking indivisible positions, therefore, will fall to the eldest; if there is no economic or social "frontier" which provides opportunities for the younger sons to make their own way, each position remains subordinate to the brother next oldest throughout life.

Because of the prominence of genealogical conceptions of succession to offices and ranks in chiefdoms, genealogies are more accurately calculated and for a greater number of generations than in tribes or bands. This is particularly true, of course, for people of high rank because they are more interested in their eminent ancestors than are people of lowly birth. Polynesian chiefs are said to have been able to calculate their genealogies for as far back as fifty generations. Nevertheless, considerations of birth order tend to dominate most chiefdoms at every social level, from the status of individuals in a family to the relations of families to others, kin group to kin group, and so on.

The basic ordering of society, then, is hierarchical. The society is composed of individuals, families, kin groups or villages, and lineages which are unlike each other. The relations, expectations, forms of etiquette, frequently even the kinds of dress and ornamentation prescribed for each extend, make explicit, and emphasize social differences.

There is an apparent tendency among chiefdoms to use sumptuary rules not only to separate individuals hierarchically but also to separate two or more generic social categories—"classes"—of people. The word "class" has had ambiguous usage, however, so let us be careful. In one sense of the word, classes exist when an *objective* stratification in the society appears which includes whole families in each stratum. In another sense, classes exist when the people in the society *think* they exist, whether or not they are particularly objective as socioeconomic entities. The class society of feudal Europe is a good example of the first kind. There were peasants who worked the land and aristocrats who owned (or controlled) it and did not work, a division accompanied by enormous differences in wealth and culture. (The so-called "middle class" was a sort of residual category of such people as craftsmen and merchants who did not fit into the two-class system.) The classes of the primitive chiefdoms were not of this sort; there was no such clear economic division between the strata. The social ranking of chiefdoms even subdivided families and frequently formed a continuous gradation from top to bottom. As one ethnographer put it with respect to the Nootka, "if they have classes, then everyone is in a class by himself." They tend to be graded internally like a feudal aristocratic class, but with no mass of peasants underneath.[3]

It is interesting that many well-developed chiefdoms seem to have had a *conceptual* class division. In fact, certain measures were often taken to create or accentuate distinctions which were artificial, in a sense, rather than being based on a true economic dichotomy as in feudal society. The Tahitians, for example, named the chiefs *Ari'i,* the general "aristocracy" the *Ra'atira,* the others *Manehune.* The Central Asian herders' *Bone* (meaning consanguineal relationship) was of two kinds of people, *White Bone* (aristocrats) and *Black Bone* (commoners). The Natchez and some other American Indian chiefdoms had a conception of *Sun People, Nobles,* and *Stinkards.* The differences between the two (or three) kinds of personages in the society were created and emphasized by forbidding one kind to eat, drink, speak, sing, and behave generally in ways distinctive of the other. Actual economic classes have great significance for the so-

---

[3] For a good discussion of the rank versus class question see Codere (1957).

cial analysis of society in later stages, but so also do these conceptually created classes.

Rules of behavior that will create apparent classes of people have important political functions. By cutting across families and local kin groups or villages with this device the society as a whole becomes stronger and more easily governed. The use of sumptuary rules for this purpose is readily seen in any modern army. There is in the U. S. Army a continuous gradation of rank from private, corporal, sergeant, lieutenant, on to the five-star general. But a sharp break is made in the continuity of the gradation by emphasizing the distinction between "officers" and "men." Sumptuary rules in dress, ornamentation, and privilege are made, and rules of etiquette ("military courtesy") help create a social distance which might be called "artificial daylight" between the two classes. As everyone must know, the purpose of this is clearly and explicitly to implement authority.

Chiefdoms have centralized direction and problems of governance, but no true government to back up decisions by legalized force. It may be that for this reason sumptuary rules and the emphasis on rank come to such a sudden prominence at the chiefdom stage in the evolution of culture. This point should be emphasized, for there has been a tendency in modern thought to see exploitation, wealth expropriation, greed, as causes of the rise of authority, classes, and the state. However, this view is manifestly erroneous if we consider chiefdoms to be a stage in social evolution occupying the position intermediate between tribal society and civil society. Sumptuary rules, particularly in food, dress, and other matters of consumption, clearly do not have their origin in economic self-seeking; the classes are in origin social and political, not economic. In fact, the sumptuary rules of many chiefdoms often so handicap and limit the behavior of the chiefs and aristocrats that they obviously are not valued for the enjoyment of their intrinsic qualities but for the prestige they carry.

It is perhaps difficult to imagine how the creation of separate bodies of people could be a socially integrative device, and truly it would not be if the separation were on a local basis with the groups each having a large measure of economic self-sufficiency. But horizontal stratification, it should be remembered, cuts directly across kin groups, villages, and other kinds of local communities, and thus binds them together in new ways. It is as relevant and significant to think of society—any society—as being a resultant of the *separations* within the total body as of the *union* of individuals; these are twin aspects of the single process of society-building.

The people of the upper stratum of a chiefdom are ranked with respect to each other in terms of their hereditary authority roles. But, as mentioned before, the authority is not backed by a state with its monopoly of force. It is appropriate now to discuss this peculiar kind of authority; rules would seem to have something to do with it. We are accustomed in industrial-urban society to think of authority as resting on some form of power, and power ultimately depends on some ability to coerce by force. But authority exists as a very strong element in chiefdoms, and there the situation is very different.

Hannah Arendt (1961) has given a description of authority that may be useful here:

> Since authority always demands obedience, it is commonly mistaken for some form of power or violence. Yet authority precludes the use of external means of coercion; where force is used, authority itself has failed. Authority, on the other hand, is incompatible with persuasion, which presupposes equality and works through a process of argumentation. . . . The authoritarian relation between the one who commands and the one who obeys rests neither on common reason nor on the power of the one who commands; what they have in common is the hierarchy itself, whose rightness and legitimacy both recognize and where both have their predetermined stable place [pp. 92–93].

Some of the economic and situational circumstances which could have been selective for the rise of individuals to important positions with respect to economic redistribution have been discussed. Collection and allocation of goods through a chief clearly can benefit most of the people involved. The person who occupies the position probably did so, originally, on the basis of some amount of public consensus; he could have been backed, so to speak, by a majority which could use force, if necessary. At this point he may have had some coercive power but no authority, in Arendt's usage, for his position was not yet part of a structured hierarchy whose "rightness and legitimacy" was recognized.

When, however, this position becomes stabilized by strict rules of hereditary succession and sanctioned by mythology, custom, values, and so on, then to the extent that these are strong and consistent so is the authority strong and consistent. The concept of a truly stable, fully structured chiefdom is necessary to our understanding, but we should realize that it is an idealization; not all chiefdoms were characterized by fully hereditary authority positions. For example, the Polynesians who settled New Zealand found a wide-open environment to expand into, so that frontier-like pioneering was possible and a leader of low hereditary position could nevertheless by charismatic force gain a following and raise his status by achievement in carving out a new domain. Thus the Maori of New Zealand have been described as more "democratic" than most of the other Polynesian chiefdoms. Samoa has also been described as allowing for achievement as a criterion of rank.

Complete stability with completely hereditary succession to office goes with a chiefdom of relatively closed resources and a population balanced with respect to them. Whatever disturbs this balance throws open some of the offices or allows for new ones. When a falling off of population, combined with European commerce and the possibility of new

forms of leadership—as in parts of Polynesia and the Northwest Coast—opened noble ranks for succession by achievement, a great efflorescence of status rivalry took place.

But even when there was some instability in the chiefdom
and individual achievement in gaining office was possible,
the new encumbents seem to have been required continuously to validate themselves in this position. As they did so,
of course, they strove to make succession hereditary; and it
appears that the conception of office was that it *was* (ought
to be) hereditary even when in fact it could be achieved at
times by effort. In such social situations modes of marriage
and postmarital residence may be altered; the ways in which
they are altered reveal the nature and significance of marriage and residence rules with respect to a more stable chiefdom.

In connection with marriage and residence, there is the
possibility of tribal-like customs existing residually after
being partially overcome, or at least modified, by the influence of ranks and new kinds of genealogical conceptions. In
particular, although exogamy of residential groups, unilocal
residence, and related conceptions of lineality may continue
in chiefdoms with some degree of effectiveness, they may be
ignored or abrogated many times by the form of marriage
which dictates endogamy within categories of rank. Endogamy would be particularly likely, in a stable chiefdom, at
the higher ranks; the higher up the pyramid the more important is this consideration and the fewer the choices. A
high-ranking boy might marry a girl of his own residential
group—thus possibly a close relative—simply because he
might have no choices of the desired rank from another
residential group. To the extent that local exogamy is given
up in favor of endogamy by rank, the character of residential groups is altered toward the cognatic type.

Another trait fairly frequent in chiefdoms, as in higher
levels of social organization, is what Firth (1957) has called
"optative" affiliation. This means that the newly married

couple have some choice as to which of the parental groups they will affiliate with, ordinarily, where they will reside. In chiefdoms it would mean simply that they are likely to choose to affiliate with whichever group confers on them the highest rank. This practice is not unfamiliar to us. For example, a European nobleman who has no son, or no willing or competent son, to leave his title and estate to may arrange to leave the inheritance to his daughter's husband. Such circumstances occur most often, of course, in times of declining population, of which Polynesian and Northwest Coast history furnish examples.

Ordinarily the man thus taken into his wife's group inherits the title (or name) of the father-in-law in due time as well as the office or rank; hence this may appropriately be seen as a form of adoption. Sometimes anthropologists have described this situation from the point of view of a child of such a marriage and called it matrilineal, but it clearly is not. The child's mother provides, by her marriage, a linkage of sorts to her own line while the child's father's line may be ignored in favor of it, but this is a linkage to her *patrilineal* line—that is, succession and/or inheritance, not descent, is involved and the descent lines of the child's father and mother both remain patrilineal or cognatic or whatever they were. Sometimes when such transference from one line to another by optative marriage is frequent enough to be noticeable as an alternative, the term "ambilineal" has been used. This term is all right if inheritance or succession is all that is meant. Unfortunately, however, the word has usually been applied to the descent groups themselves. Clearly a descent group cannot be ambilineal any more than it can be a double-descent group; it can ambiguously, or optionally, or otherwise variously *affiliate* individual persons to itself, but as a descent group it must remain matrilineal, patrilineal, cognatic, or not a descent group at all. The "ambi-ness" pertains only to an individual when he faces the choice of which group to affili-

ate with. This is not to say that such flexibility in affiliation
has no effect on descent conceptions or on the nature of
the groups themselves, for it does, but we must guard against
confusing the two.

Other kinds of conceptions which arise in chiefdoms, very
different from those discussed so far, are nevertheless closely
related to matters of descent, marriage, inheritance, and
affiliation. These have to do with genealogy, more particularly, with the naming of genealogical categories. The names
are sociocentric and are not considered by the ethnologist,
ordinarily, as a part of the kinship system; thus titles of
office and names of descent lines seem like *personal* names,
but they are not egocentric like personal kinship terms.

In chiefdoms, ranks are general and widely horizontal;
they are also specific and precise. A noble is thus, in certain
social contexts, also a particular *kind* of noble. Inasmuch
as these specific ranks are individual and inherited by primogeniture, they proliferate as the genealogy of individual
birth-order positions proliferates. At higher levels of the
society, if not in the whole society, these ranks are named
as positions and that name, or one associated with it, also
becomes a status term in social interaction. But such a position is not only a status term and a personal identification,
but also a name for a branch or bud in the genealogical tree.

The conception of descent, then, becomes not merely one
of common descent with others from shared ancestors, as
in tribal society, though such a general conception may remain. In this conceptually understood descent system there
is a main line of first-born sons of first-born sons, a line of
first-born sons of second-borns, second-born of second-born,
and so on. This is the so-called cone-shaped genealogy. Descent, in these terms, reflects the unequal ranks of all contemporaneous descendants of the founder. In another sense,
it can be said that the system uses completely denotative
conceptions of relationship.

SOCIAL STRUCTURE

Demographically, the level of chiefdoms is in part a continuation of the trend noted in the transition from band to tribal society, an increase in density of the whole society and often, also, an increase in the size of the individual residential groups. The configuration of the society as a whole and its integrative means, however, are distinctive, just as the integrative means of tribal society are different from those of bands.

Tribes are integrated by pan-tribal sodalities but chiefdoms are not, though, like bands, they may have a few minor sodalities for limited special purposes. It would seem that clans, secret societies, warrior and curing societies, and the like become less significant in well-developed and stable chiefdoms than in tribes simply because their integrative functions, and even their special purposes, often, have been rendered less necessary by the solidary organic nature of chiefdoms. There would be cases, of course, of disordered large chiefdoms which would need sodalities for special purposes. Even some African states have several sodalities of the tribal sort.

Local residential groups theoretically could be of several different kinds. Their nature could differ depending on whether the society was of herders, sedentary agriculturalists, fishermen, or varying combinations of these, and also depending on the original nature of the groups before the society became a chiefdom. But it should be remembered that in a typical chiefdom the residential group is no longer the relatively autonomous and self-sufficient economic and sociopolitical entity that it was in tribal society. Furthermore, there is a tendency for different residential groups to specialize and to become increasingly unlike each other not only in such things as rank but in their economic nature.

However, the amount of specialization of this kind, too, is variable.

Two main demographic surmises could be made. The obvious one, to repeat, is that in most cases the residential groups could be larger than those of tribes and, of course, of bands. The actual size and shape of the group, however, would depend on such things as defensive arrangements, relative economic sedentariness, and so on. The second expectation is that although the chiefdom may have been made up of lineal groups originally, there is a tendency for such groups to become somewhat cognatic through time as marital residence rules become less strictly unilocal, more optative with respect to considerations of rank and the inheritance of it. Inasmuch as such considerations are more likely at the higher ranks, a difference in the makeup of particular residential groups may arise. If, for instance, the residential groups are lineages but some are of higher rank than others, then the higher lineages will have more of a mixed, or cognatic, character than the lower. The very highest might, in time, become fully endogamous as marriage possibilities to outside groups become ever more restricted and as preservation of the high family rank and prerogatives dictates closer in-marriages.

A further characteristic of the spatial distribution of residential groups is that a well-developed chiefdom that expands territorially through internal population growth tends to do so through a process quite distinct from that of bands or tribes. These latter societies expand in an area by fissioning, creating additional groups which largely replicate each other. Chiefdoms, on the other hand, tend to expand by a sort of budding off of families that have low potentiality in the inheritance scheme. Typically, the youngest brothers are those who found their families in the new areas. To the extent that the spatial distribution of growth is unimpeded, there is a tendency for distance from the original center to correspond to rank differences among the local groups and to genealogical distance calculated in terms of the pervasive mode of primogeniture. In other words, there arise ranked minimal groups within maximal groups, thus giving the society itself, as well as the descent-reckoning system, the cone-shape that Kirchhoff (1955) considered a primary indicative characteristic.

Firth (1936) suggested the designation *ramage* for this kind of kin-group alignment which arises through "the branching and rebranching of the family structure, acquiring greater autonomy and independence the further they move away from the parent stem" (p. 371). The word has since been variously redefined, but Firth's original definition is appropriate for the style of kinship residential grouping described above.

Only some chiefdoms, of course, are fully characterized from top to bottom by the pyramidal ramage, for not all presumably grew and spread as a result of internal pressure. Yet there is a tendency for rank conceptions to intrude themselves on new groups and on the lower orders when the growth is by accretion. Sometimes, we may suppose, emulation of the aristocracy occurs, and at other times the aristocracy may impose its conceptions on all residential groups no matter the disposition of the people concerned. In all cases, at any rate, the chiefdom places a sort of umbrella over the whole society so that no one can be in doubt as to his *membership*, if not his precise place, in it.

This point is of some significance for an evolutionary view of sociopolitical forms. The succession of these forms may be seen not only as a difference in scale, shape, and kind of integration, but also the integration may result in a difference in what might be called the *distinctness and permanence* of the sociopolitical body.

Bands, it may be recalled, are integrated above the level of residential groups only by individual affinal kinship alliances. Rarely are boundaries to this ordering very clear;

there is a shading off, with distance, to more and more unlike people. The number of people that are mustered for
political purposes is never of any constant size, for it fluc-
tuates greatly, depending on the undertaking. It is consequently difficult, if not impossible, to say what is in fact the
constant political unit in band society above the level of
the residential group. Tribes, however, are more firmly integrated by sodalities; hence, the limits of the supraresiden-
tial political unit are ordinarily more apparent. Even so,
complications arise and variations are encountered depending on what political function is being undertaken. A tribe
is still a more loosely integrated and more variably constituted entity than a chiefdom. But a chiefdom has centralized authority and a ramification of subsidiary, connected
authority that extends toward the boundary of the society;
there seems to be less fluctuation in its size according to the
particular kind of endeavor, for participation is not a voluntary matter based on variable sentiments, reciprocal agree-
ments, and the like. Chiefdoms seem to have boundaries or
borders. Territoriality or at least some criteria of membership in the society which are not based merely on sentiments
of kinship and voluntary association seem to be emerging
at the chiefdom level. If one accepts Sir Henry Maine's view
of political evolution, then chiefdoms are nearing the civili-
zational ordering in the sense that what he called the "territorial tie" of civil society is apparent, if inchoate.

STATUSES

It has already been averred that the rise of broad strata as
well as particular social positions, all of unequal rank, are
characteristic of chiefdoms. It is perhaps obvious that these
are also status positions, since a primary consideration in
all status positions (even age-sex statuses) seems to be their
relation to superordination-subordination with regard to

interpersonal behavior. The words "rank" and "stratification," of course, explicitly connote high-low orderings,
hence they may be expected to be candidates for interpersonal status usage. These would seem to be the most noticeable of the statuses specifically characteristic of chiefdoms.
A more general characteristic of chiefdoms is the much
greater number of sociocentric statuses and a fairly usual
decrease in the complexity of egocentric terminology.

Simply because chiefdoms are larger and more complex
than tribes, a commensurate increase in the number of
sociocentric status terms might be expected. This seems
clearly to be so: there are terms for warriors of varying
achievements, occupational specialties, political titles, terms
referring to group memberships (for example, "house-
names"), and a great many others which signify any of the
above elements but which are bestowed on particular individuals. These last-named are used much like proper
names although they clearly have status content as though
they were titles.[4]

It may be apparent from the above examples that nonfamilistic sociocentric statuses probably become increasingly
numerous in chiefdoms. On the one hand this could be expected because of the greater size and complexity of the
society, particularly as more areas of achievement (in warfare and crafts, for example) are possible. Unless the inherited rank is high, these achieved statuses may be used
instead of either kinship terms or title of rank. (One is
tempted again to exemplify this situation by referring to
the British aristocracy. In one sense Winston Churchill was
a member of the *upper class*, but it should be repeated that
class of this kind does not have its counterpart in chiefdoms.
Within the aristocracy and in the uses of titles and calcula-

---

[4] See particularly Swanton's discussion (1946, pp. 671–674) of names
among the Indians of Southeastern United States. See also Edmonson's
correlation of what he calls "achieved and associational statuses" with
cultural complexity (Edmonson, 1958).

tions by primogeniture, which *are* similar to chiefdoms, Churchill was a commoner even though he was the son of a Lord and descendant of a Duke. His status became an achieved one when he was dubbed Knight and thereafter called Sir Winston.)

It may also be supposed that a greater use of sociocentric status terms, particularly those of general political significance, whether achieved or ascribed, familistic or nonfamilistic, would result in less frequent use of the egocentric kinship terms, and in a more restricted range for them. This has been said to be true of Fiji (Sahlins, 1962, p. 159) and Polynesia generally (Goldman, 1955, pp. 691–692) and there is at least the implication that it is somewhat true for chiefdoms in the Southeastern United States (Swanton, 1946) and Asiatic steppe-pastoralists (Krader, 1955).

Among a great many chiefdoms, and seemingly all of the well-developed ones such as those of Polynesia and British Columbia, the egocentric terminology is of the very simple generational pattern. This would seem to be related to the probability that statuses of rank in particular, and perhaps others, have overridden statuses based on degrees of kinship within generations, so that all that remains are sex-age discriminations whenever intimate, personal relations are the context.

THE CHIEFDOM LEVEL OF SOCIOCULTURAL INTEGRATION

If our original assumption that grand differences in the general social complexity of culture will be accompanied by differences in other aspects of the culture has any validity, then certainly chiefdoms should contrast clearly with tribes in economics, art, religion, polity, and other respects.

The economic contrast has been sufficiently discussed for present purposes in relation to the rise of authority positions: central collection followed by redistribution, as opposed to direct exchanges by reciprocity. Such a systemic and coordinated indirect exchange not only makes for greater efficiency of labor but also for directed deployment of labor. The effect on technology, arts and crafts, and material culture generally is therefore potentially great. Craftsmen of superior skills can become fully subsidized so that many items of greatly superior workmanship tend to characterize chiefdoms, in contrast to tribes. The direction of public labor also leaves highly visible results: in some chiefdoms, irrigation works and terracing of slopes; in others, temples and temple-mounds, pyramids, and other such monuments.

Religion in chiefdoms is markedly different from that of tribes and bands. It is not so much that the antecedent religion is altered, but rather that it is augmented in content and with new forms superimposed. The shamanistic practices and local life-cycle rituals remain, but ceremonies and rituals serving wider social purposes become more numerous. Supernatural beings come to include ancestors in genealogical rank-order, reflecting the social order. The so-called "ancestor worship" relates to great, as opposed to lesser, ancestors—who thus resemble Gods rather than mere spirits and vague culture heroes.

Related to all this are new kinds of religious practitioners who may be said to form a priesthood. Whereas a shaman achieves his position by personal qualifications, a priest occupies a permanent office in the society. The differences between these two resemble the differences between the occasional leader of tribal society and the true chief. Chieftainship and priesthood, in fact, seem to arise together as twin forms of authority, distinct with respect to the contexts in which the authority is wielded but otherwise similar, if not identical. Ordinarily priestly offices descend in the same family line as the secular offices; further, sometimes the priest and chief are the same person. For this reason many chiefdoms have been called theocracies with considerable appropriateness.

But in an important sense polity in chiefdoms is still primitive; that is, chiefdoms are examples of kinship society rather than civil society, although the polity contrasts with that of tribes and bands in several respects. As mentioned, there is usually a more discernible boundary to a chiefdom as a consequence of the extension of legitimatized authority. Feuding is more restricted and internal strife of any kind reduced because of the mediation of authority.

To make the nature of the political order of chiefdoms clearer it will be helpful to contrast it not only with that of tribes and bands, but also with the later state organization. A true state, however undeveloped, is distinguishable from chiefdoms in particular, and all lower levels in general, by the presence of that special form of control, the consistent threat of force by a body of persons legitimately constituted to use it. Personal force, as in feuding, may be found at all levels, but in states it is the monopoly of only certain persons. Monopoly of force, as opposed to the power of a chief, for example, who might if necessary hold an *advantage* of force, is important; one of the simplest but most notable indices of a state's power lies in the degree to which personal (nongovernmental) use of force is outlawed and thereafter prevented. The presence of feud signifies the absence of state power at that time and place.

States can be socially differentiated from chiefdoms in other ways as well. One of the most striking characteristics is the division of the society into political classes. Chiefdoms have differences in individual rank and often the society is conceptually differentiated into two or three broad social strata, like the Tahitian *Ari'i, Ra'atira,* and *Manehune,* but these are social in origin, and do not arise from political or economic class differentiation. The degree of social distinction is fostered by sumptuary rules; certain items of dress, ornamentation, perhaps kinds of food, are reserved for one stratum and tabooed to the other. Sumptuary rules continue in primitive states but the classes become an aspect of full bureaucratic as well as social differentiation. Thus in states the aristocracy are the civil bureaucrats, the military leaders, and the upper priesthood. Other people "work." Full-time professionalization in arts and crafts and sometimes in commerce develops also, and people who follow these professions can be regarded as still another class.

At this point it may be well to digress briefly in order to make explicit the way in which the present classification departs from older evolutionary ideas. The discrimination of chiefdoms as a stage in cultural evolution has not been made in other evolutionary schemes and, as a consequence, there has been a great deal of confusion and argumentation with respect to the characteristics of such societies as the Polynesians or the Indians of the northwest coast of North America and in the Circum-Caribbean area.

Most of the evolutionists of the nineteenth century demarked two major stages in evolution, like Morgan's *societas* and *civitas*—kinship (or primitive) society as opposed to civil (state) society. This dichotomy seems to have survived in the thought of some modern social scientists, including the anthropological evolutionists Childe and White. The twofold distinction involves several related assumptions: *societas,* in contrast to *civitas,* is a form of society which is *familistic, egalitarian,* without *government,* without *private property* or *entrepreneurs* or a *market,* and without *socioeconomic classes.*

What, then, are the societies we have called chiefdoms? A chiefdom is largely familistic but is not egalitarian; it has no government but does have authority and centralized direction; there is no private property in resources or entrepreneurial market commerce, yet there is unequal control over goods and production; there are rank differences but no clear socioeconomic or political classes. Despite the fact that chiefdoms are numerous and are found widely separated on the globe, they have not been set off as a distinct form of society, significant in their own right. Rather, descriptions and interpretations of several chiefdoms have varied tremendously, depending on whether the investigator thinks of them as examples of *societas* or as early civil states.

The redistributional economy, particularly, being unfamiliar and unnamed as a distinctive form of economic organization, has caused great discrepancies among the writings of such peoples. The movement of goods from the producers *to* the center is sometimes described as "taxes," "tribute," or "exploitation" of the "masses" by the heavyhanded "king." Yet other writers can see the same society as an example of "primitive communism" by paying more attention to the movement of goods *from* the center to the grateful populace. One interpreter may see the internal ranking based on genealogy as indicative of a class-ridden, despotic state; yet another writer may note that the society is based on kinship and thus there can be no true classes.

The simplest way out is to define these societies in their own terms. Chiefdoms are chiefdoms and states are states. States retain many of the characteristics of chiefdoms—each successive stage of evolution incorporates many aspects of the previous stage—but the new form of integration is the emergent feature and is thus definitive. A state is unlike a chiefdom because it is integrated by a special mechanism involving legitimatized force. It constitutes itself *legally:* it makes explicit the manner and circumstances of its use of force and forbids other use of force by lawfully interfering in disputes between individuals and between corporate parts of the society (Fried, 1967).

As originally planned, the discussion of evolution and social organization should have ended here. The book was supposed to be a small one and also, inasmuch as it is directed to anthropology students, it seemed appropriate to restrict the contents to the primitive levels of society which have been the primary focus of anthropology. "Primitive," of course, can be defined in a number of ways. It would be consonant with most earlier uses to restrict it to the pre-state, or precivilizational levels. It seemed a good place to stop, also, because the most profound division that can be discerned in the total evolution of culture, particularly in terms of the social criteria used here, is that between the primitive, or *societas*, kinds of cultures (including chiefdoms) and civilization.

It is hard to leave it at that, however. One of the most interesting and important of all the problems anthropology faces is how to fill in the picture factually and bridge the gap theoretically between our comprehension of primitive culture and the beginnings of civilization. One way of starting a discussion of this matter is to ask a few simple related questions: What *is* the next stage? How could its characteristics be defined? How many more stages are there? What kind of stage lies between chiefdoms and full-fledged Classical or Archaic Civilization? The stages of Bands, Tribes, and Chiefdoms were characterized with what may have seemed like an air of confidence: can such bravado be sustained?

The answer to the last question is no. Therefore it is with uncertainty and intellectual diffidence that we attempt, in the next few pages, to relate the criterion of organizational stages that has been employed so far to the next stage, if for no other reason than to see how it fits and thus to stimulate refinements or rebuttals.

First, with respect to the stage above chiefdoms and to the number of stages below the modern industrial state, it is apparent that there are in that area some rather grand differences among particular societies. These differences have been noted in anthropological literature. They are implicit in such terminology as "Primitive State" for such societies as Ashanti and Benin, or Inca and Aztec, for example, as opposed to "archaic" or "classical" civilizations of the order of dynastic China and Mogul India, or the Greek and Roman Empires. Are these *two* stages between primitive, or prestate, society and the industrial nation-state, or one? Of course one may lump them or separate them depending on the questions asked. It will be useful to consider how they might be demarked by applying the same criterion that was used in discriminating the previous stages.

It seems plausible to argue that, despite great differences in the size, density, and complexity of archaic civilization as compared with such relatively modest states as, say, Ashanti, these are differences of degree rather than kind. The same integrative mechanism—bureaucratic governance by legal force—is operative. But inasmuch as this mechanism has enormous potentiality for integration, the differences of degree among states are also potentially enormous. Thus an archaic civilization like classical China is an example of very high development and the Inca or Aztec represent lower development within what is basically the same stage. There was much more specialization and greater size and complexity in China, but the means of integration remained generically the same.

On the other hand, the differences between the preindustrial empires (China, India, Mesopotamia, Egypt, or Rome, for example) and the less developed states have been of great interest to some anthropologists and many attempts have been made to name the distinguishing feature. The presence of writing was one of the first and remains a fairly usual criterion of the origin of civilization. V. Gordon Childe (1946) and some others have cited the economic causes of the rise of cities and called the origin of civilization an Urban Revolution. More recently Wittfogel (1957) has emphasized the association in archaic times of the urban revolution and the concomitant creation of autocratic bureaucracies with large-scale irrigation projects.

All of these factors have some significance, certainly. Increased production through irrigation, increased centralized control, increased size of cities, and an increase in communicative and notational devices—mathematics as well as writing—all tended to come about in some relation to each other. To these might be added another distinctive feature of the archaic civilizations: they were *empires,* incorporating originally diverse cultures and ethnic groups into one large civil order. Most of the societies called primitive states were more homogeneous ethnically and culturally. An exception was the Inca state, whose integration was recent at the time of Pizarro's intervention and so weak that it might not have survived the civil war that was raging.

An empire, in the above sense, is a society which incorporates many diverse cultural units, a thing which had never been done successfully in a social system at any previous level except for adoptions of individuals and piecemeal assimilation of small groups that were ethnically and culturally similar. The attraction of likeness and the repulsion of unlikeness have always been and always will be important in any social order, although alone they cannot integrate large societies. But when this attraction–repulsion factor is absent, as in an empire of discrete cultural (and/or ethnic) societies, new difficulties of integration arise. The difficulties are such, in fact, that the "fall of empires" (or better, "falling-apart") has been so recurrent that it has become a subject of historical generalization. A successful empire (one that lasts a long time) seems to be the only kind we count as archaic civilization. Thus we must take into account an integration which achieves what had apparently always been impossible before, the incorporation of distinct cultures, ethnic groups, or even linguistic groups, and which also achieves a stabilization for so long that a new kind of culture—at least in some respects—comes to characterize it.

This is to say that the problems of governance were so great that the successfully integrated empires, the classical archaic civilizations, had made great advances in jurisprudence, military science, theocracy (a religious structure as an aspect of government), bureaucracy, bureaucratic commerce, communication, and so on. Eventually these important advances, first made in the urban centers, became more pervasive and stabilized into urban and rural components, so that it is now customary to speak of the "high culture" or the "great tradition," to differentiate aristocratic and urban subculture from rural or peasant cultural aspects of the empire. Thus two classes of people tended to become two subcultures as well, cross-cutting the original local cultural differences.

The provisional judgment at this point is that archaic civilization represents the culmination of tendencies inherent in the integrative potentialities of the primitive, preindustrial state.[5] This is to say (or admit) that for consistency and neatness the "primitive state" category probably should not be set off conceptually from the archaic civilizations. In terms of the classificatory devices used here the Inca State, for example, is not qualitatively distinct from, say, classical China—it is merely a smaller, shorter-lived, much less developed example of the same *kind* of thing.

---

[5] The term "preindustrial" seems advised, for the industrial "national" state of modern times is another kind of thing. Its characteristics cannot be discussed here; however, it might be suggested that the industrial state can be considered a new stage with powerful new integrative factors residing in the tremendously complex occupational network created by industrialization.

6

Conclusions

Evolution, whether biological or cultural, is a continuum of change in that any particular form must have grown out of an ancestral form. It is also discontinuous; descendant lines diverge from each other. Evolution, in the adaptive perspective, can be described in terms of a phylogenetic (or historical) taxonomy that does not violate the actualities of continuity and discontinuity. Such a taxonomy is used precisely because of this interest; ancestrally related forms are labeled as such and are thus distinguished from divergent lines.

But it should have been noticed by now that despite considerable discussion of such evolutionary movements, the arrangement of chapters in this book has been in terms of a classification that is not historical. Bands, tribes, and chiefdoms are levels or stages of a general, not a specific, adaptive-historical perspective, and certain arbitrary criteria are employed which allow the inclusion of *unrelated* societies in a class. The assumption is that a few criteria, if appropriate, are indicative of some degree of general similarity among the societies. Thus structural convergence is the focus of interest in the general evolutionary classification; at the same time, linear divergence is recognized in the specific adaptive view.

If one or a few criteria of classification are believed to imply other important characteristics of the type, then of course the classifier is some sort of functionalist. An important virtue of the evolutionary classification, however, is that the classifier need not be a functionalist by faith alone, for there are ways by which the notions of functional necessity can be tested. The very classification itself is also testable for utility in that it should "hold" the data and render them more intelligible. Particularly, it should hold new data not included in the original classification.

All classifications are arbitrary, but this does not mean that they are therefore equal. One is better than another if it is more useful. To be useful a scheme of general evolutionary classification has implications with respect to functional necessity, developmental priority ("cause-and-effect" in the common-sense meaning of the terms), and various other significances. A classification means something.

There are also some things that a classification does not mean. There has been a tendency to assume that the aspects of culture used as criteria in the discrimination of stages, or in any other classification of types on a nonphylogenetic basis, are therefore also "prime movers," "core features," "diagnostic," or "basic." Thus it is L. A. White's belief that the amount of energy harnessed by a society is fundamental and that technological changes are the prime movers in accomplishing increases in amount of energy harnessed and in determining other cultural characteristics. Consequently, he classifies cultures into a human-energy or wild-food stage, a stage of plant-animal domestication, and a fuel-energy stage. Ruth Benedict placed emphasis on psychology and ideology as determinants of types of culture and she classified the types as Apollonian, Paranoid, and Dionysian.

Marxians classify societies economically, because of the presumed basic determining effect of economics on other aspects of culture.

But what do we mean by "basic"? Basic for what? The
criteria used in this book as discriminators of stages are
social-structural, and one aspect of social structure, the
form of integration, is given special prominence as the
prime indicator. Does this mean that social structure in
general, and integrative means in particular, are somehow
prime movers or basic causes of something?

If the terms "basic" or "prime mover" refer to aspects of
culture that have developmental priority, or are determinants or causes of other things in the context of evolutionary change, then we are considering the process of
change—how and in what order changes actually take place.
Even if this is done only inferentially or imaginatively it
must refer to particular cultures in real environments, with
attention to the prior ingredients and the adaptive situations. This is of course specific evolution. But it does not
follow that those aspects of culture that have some priority
in determining other things when changes take place must
necessarily be those that are used in classifying stages in
general evolution. An *indicator* is not of necessity a *determinant* of anything; it can as well have been precipitated
out of the change as stabilization takes place while the
original prime mover recedes in significance.

Thus the fact that social-structural criteria are used here
as indicators for classes of societies says nothing about their
role as *causes* of growth and complexity. Social structure,
as a matter of fact, would seem to be a result of the workings
of other factors and the cause of nothing. These criteria
were chosen simply because we are concerned here with
the problem of degrees of complexity of society. This is not
to say that an evolutionary view requires that the simple-
to-complex line of social structures must constitute the ordering. I have chosen this ordering because social organiza-

tion is our present subject matter, and a consideration of relative complexity seems helpful in comprehending it.

Simply stated, greater complexity means more parts, and more parts will require more effective integration of the whole which accommodates the parts. If this is so, then it may well be that the form of integration alone will imply the rest, that it may be taken as a measure of the degree of complexity. It may also denote a *kind* of complexity.

Subdivision or segmentation—the creation of more parts and the increasing differentiation of them—must have been, like growth itself, a gradual process, however variable in pace from one specific habitat to another. But the means by which these parts are integrated were probably not so gradually evolved. An increase in size and density, and multiplication of parts in the social body, can go on gradually under the same integrative means only up to the point where those means fail to do the job. After that a society must fission into two or more separate societies if growth continues. This separation probably happened over and over again in history. Only if *new* integrative means are added can an increase in complexity accompany the growth. Thus while growth is a continuum, the succession of means of integration must be discontinuous.

It would seem that qualitatively distinct means of integration are few in human society. They appear to be five in number, although it is possible to think of subvarieties of each: (1) familistic bonds of kinship and marriage which by their nature can integrate only the relatively small and simple societies that we call bands; (2) pan-tribal sodalities which can integrate several bandlike societies into one; (3) specialization, redistribution, and the related centralization of authority which can integrate still more complex societies; (4) the state, further integrated by a bureaucracy employing legal force; (5) an industrial society integrated not only by a state apparatus but also by a complex network of specialized, interdependent occupations.

Only the first three of these have been used in this book, and not enough data were brought together to make a good test of the usefulness of the assumptions that underlie them. Further tests should be made with a large and broad sample of primitive societies which, when separated into the three categories of complexity, would reveal the extent to which the assumptions reflect reality.

First of all, if the forms of integration described in the classification are in fact qualitatively distinct rather than continuously linked, and if they are in fact necessary to an appropriate size and complexity of the society, then the three classes of societies should actually appear as distinct levels. That is, there should be "daylight" between each class in the sense that many societies should be clustered at each level and fewer ranged in between them. At the same time the assumptions about internal functional necessity are testable. If there *are* actually three clusters, it would be a simple matter to discover what aspects or traits of culture go together. If the societies form a continuous gradation instead of clusters, then rank-ordering, scaling, or some such more sophisticated method could be used.

These tests have not been made. The present book is only a crude beginning, little more than an argument in favor of hypotheses, for an enormous amount of work lies ahead. The classifications cannot be tested now with any rapid and broad statistical study of data from cross-cultural files, but only after there are many more ethnohistorical studies of the sort that will enable us to disentangle aboriginal primitive societies from those so drastically altered by modern influences. The classification of the societies must be based on the assumption that they are bands adapted to other bands, tribes to tribes, and chiefdoms to chiefdoms.

A considerable effort was made during the preparation of this book to make a preliminary discrimination of aboriginal from modernly reconstituted societies in order to have something to begin with. Most of this effort was given to the band level because there had been a tendency for many of us (including myself) to accept in too simple a form Steward's compelling ecological theory of composite bands. This has confused our thoughts about evolution as well as the very classification of stages. However, as the ethnohistorical work summarized here progressed, the issue seemed more and more to be resolved in favor of the present evolutionary assumptions. But there should be no complacency about this; more work may well change the picture.

It should be understood that the emphasis on discriminating aboriginal culture from disrupted and readapted societies was necessary for the special purposes of this book, and it is not meant to imply that the latter are scientifically unimportant. The reconstituted societies are not relevant in an ethnographic sample for general evolutionary classification, but many important problems remain for which they are relevant. Acculturation, or readaptation, should be of great interest for its own sake, and there is already a considerable body of anthropological studies of acculturation, especially concerning North American Indians, and a growing sophistication about the varying kinds and means of readaptation and about the conditions that cause them. They are not summarized or discussed in all their variety, however, for that would take us too far from our purpose.

Now, admitted that the present arrangement of data to the form of classification is in no sense conclusive, there are some suggestions, nevertheless, that derive from it. As stated before, a classification means something. The most important meaning of any classification made from a developmental point of view has to do with the matter of function.

In much of recent anthropological theory the problem of functional relationships is prejudged by using the word "system." It is almost an article of faith among most of us today that a culture is a system, a social organization is a system, a language is a system, and so on. This may have been a reaction to earlier views of culture as a "planless hodgepodge, . . . [a] thing of shreds and patches." Perhaps it is an overreaction. Many studies have shown (or argued for) the interrelationship between certain particular traits in a culture. However it does not follow that *all* parts are interrelated or even integrated, nor does it mean that there is necessarily coherence or pattern—except for that imposed by the anthropologist himself in his struggle for comprehension. What seem to be needed are more evolutionary studies designed to reveal those things that actually *are* related, for only in the course of evolutionary change are such functional connections fully revealed.

The classification of stages made here suggests two different kinds of conclusions with respect to functional relationships.

On the one hand the classification seems to show the ways in which kinship terminology is related to social structure. The equally important obverse side of this is that there are parts of kinship terminology that are *not* related to social structure or to each other. This point will be discussed in the section of this chapter titled Kinship Terminology and Social Structure.

The other aspect of the functional problem has to do with the question of developmental priorities. A classification made from a general evolutionary perspective reveals that in one stage there are some things not found in the underlying stage; that is, "developments" are discovered. How such new things come about, how they are invented, selected, and adapted to other things are questions of specific evolution, but the original ideas of what these new traits are come from the general classification. Thus both the general and specific evolutionary perspectives are useful with respect to the same problem: some specific evolutionary adaptive changes may be also developments with general significance. Divergence corresponds to progress in some cases, and a specific movement of this sort thus might be equal to a change from one stage to another. The "conjectural history" that begins each of the chapters in this book is an attempt to describe the probable order of new developmental factors that are significant in general evolutionary progress. Such concerns are the most striking characteristic of evolutionary theory as compared to the more prevalent functional theory. The final section of this chapter, Functionalism, Evolutionism, and Culture, discusses these two theories more fully with respect to their capacity for discovering developmental cause-effect relationships.

But first we must interpose a methodological point. In an important degree the conclusions reached have been due to a consistently held perspective that eschews reductionism in all of its many forms, but particularly that kind which confuses an individual's role and place in a society with an explanation of the processes of the society itself.

SOCIAL ORGANIZATION AND INDIVIDUALISM

The cliché that "it is always the individual that really thinks and acts and dreams and revolts" is frequently matched, particularly in the United States, by emphasis on the individual when social structure, economics, religion, art, and so on are analyzed. Thus in most studies of social structure (especially Murdock, 1949) there is the conception of the "primary group," usually the domestic or nuclear family, which most closely envelops a particular person; then there are secondary groups or rings of people farther away with less consistent personal influences on him. In this perspective primary group also becomes, implicitly at least, basic group and most important group. Is this because individualism is such a marked characteristic of the value system of modern entrepreneurial society?

The individualistic perspective is useful in understanding personality development, enculturation, and other questions which have to do with individuals, of course, but in the context of evolutionary questions about social organization it is the wrong end of the stick. The individual with his primary group *is* basic and important—but for certain problems only. On the other hand, a nonindividualistic, impersonal, bird's-eye view of the organization as a whole may be necessary for the solution of a different order of questions. This point is obvious enough and it should not be necessary to argue. After all, segmentation and differentiation, the formation of groups and statuses, are processes of an organization and an organization is a whole. If such processes are going on *within* a developing society, the resulting parts then cannot be regarded as the primary building blocks out of which the society was built as though by accretion.[1]

What is not obvious, however, and what therefore needs particular notice here, is the unconscious and subtle way in which the individualistic perspective has influenced analysis and explanation of status systems. This may be discussed under three headings.

1. FAMILISTIC AND NONFAMILISTIC STATUSES. Just as there has been emphasis on social structure as constellations of persons and groups radiating outward from the individual and his family of orientation, or the primary group, so has there been an emphasis on familistic, or kinship, statuses matched by a near-avoidance of consideration of nonfamilistic statuses. Here one may take Murdock's *Social Struc.ure* (1949) as an example. All of the criteria he uses in his conception of social organization are familistic. There have been rebellious mutterings in anthropology against the emphasis on kinship, and particularly against the recondite complications in the study of kin nomenclatures of status. At this point it is necessary only to say that many of the problems discussed

---

[1] Richard N. Adams has made this point convincingly (1960, p. 47).

here have such scope that a relative de-emphasis of family groups and familistic statuses was necessary, and that in the view taken the major characteristics of a social system are not regarded as sufficiently described or analyzed by a chart of the kinship terminological pattern.

2. EGOCENTRIC AND SOCIOCENTRIC STATUSES. Paralleling the usual emphasis on the individual and his related family life and familistic statuses is another common orientation. Most of the attention anthropologists give to the status network seems to be confined to what could be called *egocentric* statuses. These are the statuses that take their significance from a kind of relationship to some particular person—the "Ego" in anthropological kinship charts. *Sociocentric* statuses, on the other hand, refer to positions held in the society at large; the point of reference is not some other individual. Unlike such designations as *"my* grandfather," *"your* husband," *"Gertrude's* cook," sociocentric statuses are objectively describable with reference to groups, categories, and classes of persons of the society. There are gross, paired categories such as "young-old," "male-female," "married-unmarried," which cut entirely across the total social structure; and there are any number of more specific pigeonholes such as occupational specialties, ceremonial and political offices, ranks, and the like which can be so particularized that sometimes only one person at a time can occupy the status. But these are all alike in that the encumbent is *in* that social position no matter who is addressing or referring to him; the sociocentric status can be located on an objectified map of the social organization, so to speak, whereas egocentric statuses cannot specify who is in what status except in terms of his relation to someone else. Egocentric statuses are more personal and thus more appropriate to close-knit, face-to-face groups, varying as they do always with reference to individuals.

Kinship systems in normal anthropological usage are familistic and egocentric status nomenclatures and they have been the most important focus in the anthropological study of social life. But nonfamilistic and sociocentric statuses are important, too, and the present work has distinguished them and used them in the delineation of certain problems. Societies, large or small, are not simply families and small groups; they are also more or less complex, and complexity and forms of integration must be major subjects in evolutionary interpretation.

3. SOME ETHNOCENTRIC ASSUMPTIONS ABOUT KINSHIP. There has been a hint in the foregoing discussion that perhaps the perspective that begins with the individual might be somewhat ethnocentric in the sense that it is so typical of the home-grown ideology of modern Western civilizati n, and particularly of the United States. Certainly, in the investigation of many questions about kinship systems this seems a fair judgment. We all have been ethnocentric at times, however unknowingly.

L. H. Morgan (1871) in his earliest kinship studies found that most primitive peoples do not isolate collateral lines of descent from Ego's line as we do. In Ego's generation many primitive systems do not differentiate Ego's siblings from his cousins (or certain cousins). Similarly, in the ascendant generation father is not distinguished terminologically from father's brothers nor mother from mother's sisters and in the descending generation Ego's children are not distinguished from his nephews and nieces (or some of them). Primitive kinship systems differ at certain points, but this kind of merging of lineal and collateral lines was a common feature of most of those that Morgan studied. He gave all these a generic name, "classificatory systems," and distinguished them from our own type, which he called the "descriptive system" because it holds Ego's lineal relatives apart from collaterals.

Several implications in this dichotomy are misleading. Morgan was talking about genealogical conceptions and the ways in which the kinship systems, supposedly reflecting "blood ties," tell us about the forms of marriage and the related makeup of the family. A system "classifies" relatives when it lumps into one category people that are separated by lines of descent in the descriptive system. Any noun, of course, classifies, hence Morgan's choice of terms was poor. But aside from that, the basic issue is contained in the question: What are the criteria that made the classification? Or, to put it another way: What is it that is being described (in either system)?

Morgan's assumption that different kinds of consanguineality were the only criteria involved was challenged by McLennan and N. W. Thomas, both of whom gave cogent reasons for assuming that blood ties and descent lines were not the main criteria at all.[2] At any rate, the important question of the relationships of social groups and institutions to kinship terminology is clearly begged by the assumption that the terminologies are in fact more or less successful reproductions of the familistic social structure and its associated type of marriage and descent.

Now we come to the next question asked of the apparent fundamental dichotomy of classificatory versus descriptive kinship systems. How shall we go about explaining the differences between the two systems? Here are two polar types: a fully descriptive system separates lines of descent, crosscuts the lines by generational standing, and thus isolates persons into seemingly "natural" pigeonholes. On the other hand, the classificatory system "merges" the lines of descent,

---

[2] McLennan is usually cited, for example, by Rivers (1907), for having rebutted Morgan with the claim that kinship terms were "mere salutations," but he actually meant much more than that: the terms refer to "age and station" (1886, pp. 305, 310, and elsewhere), are a "code of courtesies" (p. 273), and show "degrees of respect" (pp. 305–306). Thomas made a similar argument against Morgan's assumptions but was more explicit in describing kin terms as denoting status and rights and duties associated with it rather than consanguineality in some direct fashion (1906, esp. Ch. 12). Andrew Lang also recommended the view that the terms denote status (1907–1908).

creating larger categories—or, in another way of putting it, this system fails to separate or distinguish certain relatives that an ideal descriptive system would isolate.[3]

It is apparently normal to human thought when confronted with such paired extremes to accept one as the more expectable, not needing explanation, and then to set about explaining the deviations of the other from that "norm." With only a few exceptions, there has been a tendency in anthropology to accept our own system as so natural that it needs no explanation (that is, it is more descriptive or denotative than most primitive systems). Our questions have been about the other system: Why are parallel cousins "merged" with siblings? Why are father's brothers called "father" and mother's sisters called "mother"? Is not this emphasis on attempting to explain the classificatory system to the relative neglect of the other a good example of unconscious ethnocentrism?

Eskimos have a large number of words for different kinds of snow: in English snow is snow. An Eastern city girl calls all cattle "cows," whereas a rancher distinguishes "heifer," "yearling," "cow," "bull," "bull-calf," "steer," and so on. In these cases one kind of person makes certain distinctions in the range of phenomena "snow" or "cows" and the other does not.

There is an analogy here to the classificatory-descriptive dichotomy in that the problem involves questions about merging things and about separating things. But how do

---

[3] A. L. Kroeber long ago (1909) criticized Morgan's contention that kinship terminologies reflect kinship institutions, but at the same time he advanced the much more dubious proposition that there are natural, or "logical," kinship categories based on eight criteria of differentiation. Hence a purely descriptive system would be denotative of all these criteria; other systems would be more classificatory as they used fewer of them. Murdock accepts this view (but with six criteria) and thus he can say: "A classificatory term can arise only by ignoring one or more fundamental distinctions between relatives which, if given full linguistic recognition, would result in designating them by different denotative terms" (1949, p. 101).

we tend to address the question? The city girl asks, "Why do ranchers have all those names for different cows?" The English-speaker wants to know, "Why do Eskimos have all those words for snow?" Here again is a kind of ethnocentrism: one's own way is normal or to be expected, and the questions are asked of the deviations away from it. But at one important point the analogy is reversed: in these examples the "normal" is classificatory, in a sense, whereas the Eskimos and the ranchers are separating things descriptively (from their point of view). The questions asked, then, are of the type, "Why are such-and-such *separations* or *distinctions* made?" In the case of the kinship dichotomy, however, the situation is reversed because of our familiarity with the descriptive system and we usually ask, "Why are those *lumpings, mergings,* or *extensions* made?"

All this is preamble to a simple point: Neither the descriptive system nor the classificatory is more normal than the other; they both need explanation. Also, the question as to why certain relatives are merged is only part of the problem. It is equally as significant to ask why certain other relatives are separated. It is true, of course, that to subdivide a totality into categories is to merge the persons in each category as well as to separate the categories from each other—these are merely two sides of the same coin. But the question usually asked is why the individuals are merged, not why the totality is subdivided. In the perspective taken here, the question was asked more frequently in the latter form because it is so rarely done.

One of our problems is that part of the ethnocentrism lies in the egocentrism of beginning with the individual and assuming that kinship categories are extended outward. We start with Ego who then has a father, mother, sister, brother, and so on in his primary group, and he calls other people by these same terms by a process of inclusion; as these others come to share certain social characteristics with the primary relatives they are assimilated by Ego into the sister, mother,

or father category. This point was made strongly by Malinowski (1913, 1930), though first by Morgan (1871, p. 470),
and has been implicit in the assumptions of most anthropologists—as indicated, for example, when they say that in
classificatory systems Ego's mother's sister is called "mother"
and father's brother is called "father," presumably because
Ego had extended the primary meanings of father and
mother outward to these other relatives.

Murdock's (1949, p. 92) phrasing of the "extensionist"
view of kinship is perhaps the clearest and most influential.
He says: "The point of departure for the analysis of kinship
is the nuclear family. Universally, it is in this social group
that the developing child establishes his first habits of reciprocal behavior." Surely this judgment applies as a "point
of departure" for an analysis of an individual's experience
and training, but he is not thereby creating any general
characteristics of the culture or social organization of the
society itself—he is merely gradually adapting himself to it.
Murdock's type of "analysis" is one of the most frequent
forms of reductionism in modern social science. (Floyd
Lounsbury [1965], a former student and colleague of Murdock's, seems the most rigidly determined of more recent
analysts of kinship to follow the extensionist view.)

A. M. Hocart (1955, p. 190), pointed out the fallacy in
the assumption that a given classificatory term like *Tama,*
which in Fijian refers not only to Ego's father but also to
all other males in that generation and moiety (that is, to
father's brothers and male parallel cousins), actually *means*
"father." *Tama* means what it designates, that given category of males. Hocart says:

> The effect on theory has been disastrous. The order in which
> we have learned the uses of *Tama* and similar words [by pro-
> ceeding genealogically from Ego to his "father"—his progenitor
> —and thence outward] has been confused with the order of
> development in actual history. Because we first took it to mean

father we slip unwittingly into the assumption that it meant father originally.

This fallacy has now received official expression in the term "kinship extensions." That expression implies that the meaning father is primary and that all other uses result from extending the term to an ever-widening circle of kinsmen.[4]

Here, perhaps, is best exemplified the fundamental difference between an individual-centered "descriptive" point of view, and a societal point of view. The questions are asked in a different form. "Why does Ego extend the status 'father' from his own father outward to other males?" is very different from asking, "Why is this body of males called *Tama* separated in status from males in the opposite moiety and of different generations?" Some new consequences result from taking this latter perspective.

KINSHIP TERMINOLOGY AND SOCIAL STRUCTURE

The question of the relationship of kinship terms to social structure has preoccupied many anthropologists since Morgan published the large compendium of terminologies called *Systems of Consanguinity and Affinity of the Human Family* in 1871. As the title indicates, Morgan thought that kinship terms were directly genealogical—that they were the names for actual, or sometimes prior, genealogical connections. His explanation of the different kinds of systems was based squarely on this assumption: if, for example, a number of men are called by the same term as Ego's progenitor, that condition must have been caused by a form of marriage of whole groups to each other, with the result that Ego did

---

[4] Raymond Firth seems to be making Hocart's argument with the remark that ". . . social process and individual behavior are not necessarily coincident, . . . ontogeny in kinship need not always recapitulate phylogeny" (1936, p. 277).

See also Epling (1967).

not know which one of the men in that group was in fact his progenitor.

Several of Morgan's contemporaries raised objections to this with sheerly factual arguments. Many peoples with classificatory systems were shown to be in no doubt as to the identity of "own" father, and actually treated him somewhat differently from others called by the same term. Also, it was pointed out, in those same systems Ego calls a group of women by the same term as that of his own mother. Would he, and others around him, be in any doubt as to who his mother was, considering how obvious pregnancy is and how long the subsequent period before weaning that is characteristic of primitive peoples? It must be that the terminology does not necessarily refer to such specific genealogical positions.

McLennan, Thomas, and Lang felt that the terms referred to status[5] and functioned in contexts of interpersonal conduct, rather than solely for purposes of genealogical identification. Such a view as this permits the *possibility* of a genealogical position coinciding with a kinship status position, as in one of the ordinary uses of our words father and mother, but with no necessary reason that it always should. Many social positions that are not genealogical have status value; many genealogical positions, on the other hand, are irrelevant to status.

Viewed this way, the question of the relation of kinship terminologies to society is somewhat altered. First of all, there seems to be no theoretical problem of the relation of status terms in general to society in general. Status positions are positions in the society which are relevant to the way a person is supposed to treat certain others and they him. In societies of different size and complexity there will be commensurately different numbers and kinds of status terms in

---

[5] McLennan, as noted earlier, did not actually use the word, but the others did, and he was clearly talking about status-like usages.

use. How many and what kinds is an empirical matter; it could be ascertained for any society, although, unfortunately, seldom done in ethnographic descriptions. There is no problem here that more work could not solve.

But this is not the way the question is usually phrased. People have argued not about status terms in general, but about "kinship systems," which are particular and special kinds of status terms. I have called them "egocentric" and "familistic" status terminologies, but I wish someone would give us some better words. Egocentric has another meaning in ordinary parlance, which is a hindrance; possibly familistic is a poor choice, too, because of the implication that the terminology originates in the nuclear family. The same objection holds for the word kinship. But let us continue their use for now since they are so established.

That the relationship of kinship terminologies to social structure is not simple and direct is obvious in the fact that some very different kinds of societies have the same kind of kinship terminology and some rather similar societies have very dissimilar terminologies. It is even more obvious when we scan the total range of cultural evolution, from simple bands to complex civilization, that kinship terminologies do not themselves evolve in any sense from simple to complex. In fact, there is no apparent directional change at all, hence kin terminology cannot be considered a reflection of the society in any direct sense.

Murdock, in his extensive comparative study of kinship and social structures, notes this lack of correlation of kinship with levels of society. He seems to conclude that the theory of evolution is therefore wrong, for he writes: "Nowhere does even a revised evolutionism find a shred of support" (1949, p. 187). L. A. White also might be cited on this question although, unlike Murdock, he firmly upholds evolutionary theory. He too notes the apparent lack of relationship of kinship terminology to evolutionary levels, but he feels that something must be wrong with our studies of kinship and not with the theory of evolution.[6]

If it be accepted that kinship terminologies are kinds of status terms, and if it be accepted that evolution typically (or, at least, often) consists of a multiplication of parts rather than total replacement of one part by another, so that the old can be retained in the new, then some important possibilities logically follow. Different kinds of status terminologies themselves may come into being successively and *directionally*, in the manner characteristic of the succession of stages in the general evolutionary perspective. Elsewhere I have suggested their successive directional rise to prominence as follows: Egocentric-familistic → Sociocentric-familistic → Egocentric-nonfamilistic → Sociocentric-nonfamilistic (Service, 1960).

For the present purpose it does not matter whether we agree on the names for these, nor even on their precise nature. It is necessary only to accept that kinship terms are subspecies of a certain kind among other possible kinds of status terms and that these different kinds come about successively. Then two theoretical matters of great significance can be discussed. One is concerned with an important characteristic of egocentric terminologies as opposed to other kinds of status terms. The second is the apparent characteristic of status terms in general that the presence of one kind can affect another even though it does not replace it. The significance of this is that kinship terminology is adapted, in certain ways, not only to social structure but also to the presence of other kinds of statuses. Let us take these two in turn.

---

[6] "Morgan's theory of the evolution of the various forms of the family and their concomitant systems of kinship has been obsolete for decades. And no one since his day has been able to work out and establish a valid theory of the evolution of kinship systems. But this does not mean that no evolution has taken place in this sector of culture" (White, 1959, p. 135).

Kinship terms are a form of egocentric nomenclature of status, though not the only one ("my Lord," for example, is egocentric but not based on kinship). Egocentric was chosen as a name for these, and sociocentric for their opposites, in order to emphasize explicitly the most important difference between the two. In egocentric terminologies the statuses are all defined in relation to a single person, an "Ego," and they include no more than what an individual knows about persons socially close enough to him to have consistent and patterned social intercourse with him. Thus only a limited number of people are involved in this social circle and only a certain number of classifications made. Sociocentric terms, on the other hand, refer to social positions in the society at large and can be in enormous number depending on the size and complexity of the society and the corresponding number of kinds of varying social contexts. An ethnologist obtains the egocentric kinship terminology of a group by asking an *individual*. He then checks it with others to see if it is the current pattern for most of the individuals in the society. This may be so, but it remains only that which each individual uses in his interpersonal circle. In a complex society, however, an ethnologist cannot find out all of the sociocentric terms pertaining to the *society* by recourse to an individual informant. Those used by a factory worker in Detroit are not identical to those of the farmer thirty miles away, nor of a Maine lobsterman, a carnival barker, physicist, movie producer, rancher, importer, hippie, or university vice-president. In other words, the totality of sociocentric statuses of a society is like a dictionary, and must be compiled similarly, because any particular individual uses only a small part of this total vocabulary of status terms and different persons use different parts of it.

An essay called "On Being Just Complicated Enough," by Anthony F. C. Wallace (1961), is pertinent here. Wallace is interested in the fact that semantic complexity in kinship "subsystems," compared by the method of componential analysis, shows no variation which correlates with the complexity of the society. Comanche kinship terminology and that of the United States were identical, for example, in semantic complexity. He then goes on to show that other taxonomic subsystems such as games (like chess, playing cards, dice), verb paradigms, phonemic alphabets, and presumably all other such things, in *any* culture, are all within a certain limit of complexity, which he argues will not contain more than 2^6 (64) entities, but of course any may contain fewer. Among the other significances attached to Wallace's "2^6 Rule" (such as the interesting matter of the definition of mental incompetents) is this: As cultures increase in complexity, they must *add* new taxonomic subsystems rather than make old ones more complex. It follows, therefore, that an increasing complexity in society is in no way "reflected" in an egocentric kinship terminology.

Wallace is talking about things—whether games, phonemic alphabets, or ego-centered kinship terminologies— that are the province of an individual's usage, that must be held in the individual's head. They not only do not grow as society grows, but cannot grow beyond certain limits. Clearly this is not to be confused with the evolution of culture. That would be almost as foolish as requiring that a conception of increase in population size must be matched by a corresponding growth in the size of the individuals in it. But is not just such a confusion of the individual with society demonstrated when Murdock says (1949, p. 187) that similarity in such things as Andamanese and Yankee ego-centered kinship systems casts doubt on the validity of stages of cultural evolution?

A closely related matter is the puzzle in the distribution of generational, or Hawaiian, kinship terminology. This is the simplest terminology of all, for relatives of Ego are distinguished in status by sex and generation only. Morgan thought that this must be the most primitive system. It is the most classificatory, hence furthest from our own, and seemed to him also closer to a social stage of promiscuity, in that anyone in the ascendant generation could be anybody's father or mother; anyone in own generation, brother or sister; and so on.

Hawaiian culture and society were not simple, however, but rather among the most complex of those ordinarily considered primitive, so that not only do we find the lack of congruence between the complexity of kinship and complexity of society that was discussed earlier, but actually the opposite. How can such a complex society as that of aboriginal Hawaii have the simplest-known kinship terminology? Further, not only is Polynesian society in general complex, but so is the family form: genealogy is traced through a great number of generations, primogeniture causes major and minor lines of descent to be delineated, ranks cross-cut them all, and so on.

This is the point of relevance of the second proposition made earlier, that an egocentric pattern may be affected by, or at certain points overcome by, other statuses. For example, the fact that one person is *Ari'i* (leader by primogeniture of a descent line) and one of his first cousins might be *Manahune* (commoner) is more important in their interpersonal dealings than their kinship relationship.[7] The fact that they are relatives of the same generation, however, is significant and can be referred to by "kin" terminology, for if they were of different generations their behavior to each other would be very different. (The status significance of differing generations, it may be suggested, is never completely overridden by other considerations in any society.) There are many other sociocentric statuses in Polynesian society which render intragenerational kinship distinctions nonfunctional: there are names of family lines which,

---

[7] Goldman notes that once in Mangareva a chief actually killed a commoner relative who addressed him by a term denoting their kinship (1955, p. 692).

though resembling surnames, also function as titles in address and reference because they are higher or lower in status with respect to each other; there are occupational specializations of great importance, like carpenter, dancer, priest, war leader, and so on. None of this means that the people do not know the difference between a brother and a cousin or father and father's brother or cousin—they can all be traced genealogically, denotatively—but that kinship terms are much less significant as statuses than are some sociocentric terms, and thus give way in usage.

From this we may derive a new hypothesis. It has been noted that a frequent consequence of disruption and acculturation in primitive society after conquest by civilization is the loss of the aboriginal egocentric pattern (for example, the bifurcate-merging), so that only simple generational terms remain. It was suggested that all that happened was the loss of bifurcation as reciprocal marriage and unilocal residence modes were given up, which had the effect of rendering affinal groups indistinct. This may be the explanation, but it would be nice to know more. On the assumption that groups of people living together will need an appropriate number of status positions, it would seem that when the residual terminology consists only of generational criteria, some others must have arisen, or been borrowed in acculturation, to function in ordering interpersonal relations. It is even conceivable that such statuses arose to prominence before the original organization completely broke down and may thus have assisted in its demise, in a sense. We do not know much about this, possibly because the new statuses would tend to be sociocentric, not kinship, and were ignored by the average ethnologist. It may be suspected, even, that imposed family names can displace aboriginal kinship terms.

There are other, more readily apparent, instances of the overriding of old statuses at certain points by later, different ones. Crow-Omaha patterns are a good case in point. They occur in societies larger than bands, and thus in societies where there are more distant relations, more numerous social contexts, and more status terms of the sociocentric kind. When lineages and clans are large and strongly corporate, the statuses associated with membership in them are of such significance that they override in usage the egocentric terminology referring to relations between the affinal groups. Thus in Ego's own lineage and/or clan his relatives are classified still on the bifurcate-merging plan, but relatives in his affinal lineage receive only the sociocentric term for their group.

To sum up the proposals concerning the relationship of kinship terminology to social structure, we may begin with the two most general points: that kinship terms are kinds of status terms and that they are egocentric. If kinship terms are status terms, then they are not simply labels for either the parts of the social structure or the genealogy of persons. Some part of the social structure may sometimes be a determinant of kinship statuses, but so are other things. And if the pattern is egocentric it is that which encloses the near relationships to an individual, unlike sociocentric statuses which are a grand total for the society at large. Thus an egocentric pattern remains always within a certain size and complexity regardless of the size and complexity of the whole society.

But none of this is to say that kinship terminologies are not related to society at all; rather it is so say that the relationship is complicated and that different aspects of society are influential in differing circumstances.

Only two criteria of social status differentiation seem to be universal. These are sex and age differences (age is ordinarily a relatively gross difference, often phrased as generational difference). No kinship terminology is without these distinctions, and a very widespread kind, the Hawaiian or generational, is composed of these alone. This is the clearest and simplest connection to be made between kinship status and society. However it is not a simple connection between social structure and kinship, in the sense that "social structure" has been used in this book. Generation and sex are biological matters that have been made cultural-social categories by the attribution of additional characteristics to them which go along with ascribed codes of conduct in interpersonal dealings. They are made into statuses.

Now all societies have age-sex statuses, hence changes in social structure, of whatever kind, will have no effect on the presence or absence of these statuses. There is no cause-effect relationship between them, only a coterminal or co-existent relationship in the sense that all societies have social structures and all have age-sex statuses.

It seems quite clear from all the evidences and cases reviewed that the point at which social structure intrudes on the pattern of kinship nomenclature is in the vertical bifurcation of the generations, and further, that certain characteristics of the social structure are determinants of where the bifurcation is encountered. Where dualism prevails between two "sides" composed of affinal groups, the status of affines to each other bifurcates generations and the widespread bifurcate-merging type of kinship terminology results.[8] Occasionally, particularly in Australia, there are marriage customs based on "semi-moieties," which separate the groups on each side which include first cross-cousins from those of more distant cross-cousins. This may affect the egocentric terminology by a further bifurcation, although ordinarily the status usage for these cases is sociocentric, as in the Australian "eight-class system." This is mentioned now

---

[8] Bifurcate-merging is used here in a rather general sense. There are variations in the terminology of sisters' and male cross-cousin's children, which are too minor and special to be reviewed at this point, but which have led some writers to classify them as separate types.

as a further example of the relationship of marriage and group relations to kinship as a cause of bifurcation.

When groups and sodalities are not exogamous and affinal to each other, as in the cases of composite and cognatic social structures, the bifurcation vanishes and the simple generational type remains. When the group structure of the society remains amorphous, but with strongly corporate functions pertaining to the individual nuclear family—as in the rugged individualism of men becoming private entrepreneurs or wage workers in the commercial fur trade, rubber-tapping, or whatever—then the terminology sometimes distinguishes this isolated nuclear family from all other relatives, who remain in generational status only. This is the so-called Eskimo pattern. It is again an example of a kind of vertical subdivision caused by a social-structural characteristic.

In more complex societies, however, we have to reckon with the influence of other kinds of status on the kinship pattern. We have already discussed the influence of lineage and clan sociocentric terms on part of the bifurcate-merging pattern to form the Crow-Omaha variations. A similar intrusion on kinship terms is the presence of more important kinds of statuses based on rank phrased in sociocentric titles, and other things, which reduce the egocentric pattern to the simple generational type again. In this connection, it may be relevant to mention the situation in the contemporary United States, where kinship terms of status seem to be going out of use altogether in much of our social life, particularly in the urban areas where occupational statuses are very important.

It seems, therefore, that three very general kinds of independent variables have determining effects on kinship terminology, not just the single one of social structure. These are (1) age-sex classifications (which are not social structures but cross-cut them) that may be thought of as horizontal; (2) social structure, the relations of families and affinal groups,

which affect vertical bifurcation; and (3) other statuses,
which influence kinship in a variety of ways, particularly
in the more complex societies.

If it is true that kinship terminologies can be affected in
one part by one kind of influence and in another part by
a different kind of influence without disturbance to the
remainder, then it follows that the complete terminologies
themselves are not made up of systemically interrelated
parts. Kinship terminologies may be thought of as patterns,
perhaps, when we compare a diagram of one kind of terminology with another, although it should be remembered that
we are making the patterns. But certainly they are not *systems,* either from the point of view of what is contained in
Ego's head or from an outside view of the components or
the behavior. The words "system" and "subsystem" were
used throughout this book because everyone else does so and
it seemed desirable not to introduce too many arguments all
at once. But at this point the judgment must be that kinship terminologies are not systems at all.

FUNCTIONALISM, EVOLUTIONISM, AND CULTURE

Once I heard a young British professor reveal his misgiv-
ings about British social anthropology. He was proud that
the followers of Radcliffe-Brown have quite properly received high praise for their ethnographies, for the way they
have revealed how parts of a given system interact, mesh,
and sometimes clash. "But," he said, "what are we to do
when the library is full of descriptions of particular social
systems? Where do we go from there? Must we build ever-
larger libraries so that we shall not finally lose our posts?"

Radcliffe-Brown, as mentor and monitor of British social
anthropology, had frequently spoken of the need for a
"natural science of society" which would eventually involve
comparisons between specific societies—a "comparative

morphology of societies." [9] More to the point of the present discussion is his prescription about evolution:

> I think that social evolution is a reality which the social anthropologist should recognize and study. Like organic evolution, it can be defined by two features. There has been a process by which, from a small number of forms of social structure, many different forms have arisen in the course of history; that is, there has been a process of diversification. Secondly, throughout this process more complex forms of social structures have developed out of, or replaced, simpler forms [1952, p. 203].

Such studies have not been made by students of Radcliffe-Brown, however, although most of his *pro*scriptions have been observed. These latter are most noticeably the taboos against the concepts "culture" and "conjectural history." It may seem curious, on the face of it, that Radcliffe-Brown suggested evolutionary study yet disavowed conjectural history and use of the concept of culture. The reason is perhaps to be found in a consideration of what he was reacting against.

Earlier in England, Tylor, Frazer, Pitt-Rivers, and other notables had conjectured a great deal and had made many comparisons among elements of culture. Ordinarily the comparative studies led to schemes of what Tylor called "evolution along its many lines." That is to say, arguments were made as to the sequential development of weapons, folktales, rituals, gods, and so on, all taken out of their local context. General stages of development of such traits and complexes were described, but very little was said about whole cultures or their social systems.

In the early part of our century the "British historical school" of Rivers, Perry, and Elliot Smith developed a theory of world-wide cultural diffusion which was also of some renown during Radcliffe-Brown's formative years, as were the theories of the German and Austrian diffusionists. In the

---

[9] See particularly the essay "On Social Structure" (Radcliffe-Brown, 1952).

United States the predominating interest was in distribution studies of culture traits revealing more limited diffusion, but even the monographs describing particular societies seemed to Radcliffe-Brown to be little more than lists of traits. He objected to all of these conceptions of culture and its history because he believed that it was necessary first to find out how *a* society functions and interrelates its elements.

We can thank Malinowski for showing in his magnificent ethnographic accounts of the Trobrianders that attention to the *wholeness* of a culture is useful to anthropological thought. Radcliffe-Brown, less through his writings than through his personal leadership of several excellent students, has made a lasting impression by a more programmatical and tighter methodological structure for functional research. Several monographs made under his spiritual aegis are among the best in world anthropology. "Structural-functionalism" was needed, and Radcliffe-Brown deserves a great deal of the credit for its development.

But these are troublous, anarchical times in American anthropology. We want to be more eclectic than before.[10] We look back from a little distance and can see the one-sidedness of past "schools of thought" and, as a result, do not want to be bound by intellectual allegiance to any of them. Yet it seems to many Americans that British social anthropology as directed by Radcliffe-Brown has had a school-like character—evidenced largely in terms of the circumscriptions, however, rather than the excellences.[11]

But now we are likely to get on dangerous, perhaps untenable, ground. It is handy to talk of "British social anthropology" sometimes, as of "French sociology," "American historicism," or the "Viennese diffusionists," but in all such generalization private injustices are committed. British social anthropologists are not all alike and as time goes on

---

[10] Goldschmidt discusses this neatly (1959, pp. 31–60).
[11] See the interesting assessment from an American's point of view by Murdock (1951) and the accompanying reply by Firth (1951).

they seem to be diverging further. Perhaps more to the point, there are also French, Dutch, and American practitioners of functionalism. Let us, therefore, not speak of national groups, nor even of individuals for the moment, but of functional*ism*, an ideal-typical form of theory and practice around which various anthropologists cluster in different degrees of proximity.

Modern functionalism has supplied what was sadly lacking in nineteenth-century anthropology. But it seems that in supplying the necessary it overreacted against nineteenth-century evolutionary theory, as did American anthropology in its own way. Because "conjectural history" and the uses of "culture" were so characteristic of, and necessary to, nineteenth-century evolutionism, they were abolished or diminished, and correlatively the kinds of questions that interested the nineteenth-century anthropologists were felt to be inappropriate.

It would seem, by analogy with biology, that modern functionalism is like anatomy. Nineteenth-century evolutionism was not; nor was it much like modern evolutionism, concerned with adaptation and diversification. But why should there be opposition between any of them? In the enormous strides biology made with the advent of evolutionary thought, anatomists, taxonomists, students of adaptation, and paleontologists all played their part. In a cultural evolutionary theory broad enough to include classification in the general evolutionary sense and studies of adaptation, specialization, and diversification in the specific evolutionary sense, to study the "morphology of societies" is not only germane but necessary. Certainly these two approaches are in no logical opposition.

Which is more important, function or ancestry? From the deep south Faulkner says, "the past is never dead, it is not even past." A famous Frenchman in America, thinking of the unprecedented society he was analyzing, said, "Since the past has ceased to throw its light upon the future, the mind of man wanders in obscurity." But Tocqueville was also, of course, fascinated with the functioning of American culture and described and analyzed it wonderfully well, as they say Faulkner does for his imaginary Yoknapatawpha County. Ancestry and function must go together if we are to understand anything fully. A division of labor is fine—nobody should stop being a functionalist or historian or whatever interests him—but the divisions should be complementary in the whole task, not antagonistic, for neither can tell more than part of the story alone.

In the development of evolutionary biology, the study of the contemporaneous life forms ("comparative morphology") was the stimulus to evolutionary theory. There was only one Neanderthal skull known to Darwin, for example; it was his collection of data on living forms that he was thinking about. In biology the ancestral relationship between birds and reptiles was posited and accepted on the basis of the comparative anatomy of the contemporary representatives alone. But how exciting it was when the fossil *Archaeopteryx* was discovered! The study of fossils did not become meaningful until evolutionary conceptions were prevalent, but then it became very meaningful. Similarly, of course, prehistoric archaeology is not very meaningful without some kind of cultural evolutionary theory (archaeologists, perhaps necessarily, seem to be somewhat immune, even in the United States, to the injunctions against evolution), and evolutionary classification itself becomes more real and meaningful as archaeology can make more and more suggestions as to the actual course of events in specific cases.

But everybody does not have to have the same special interests. It may be permissible even to say, "I don't care whether we ever have a more accurate factual record of what grew out of what—after all, it's only phylogeny." It could be argued that the record needs filling out not primarily in order to get it straight in some sense of pure history, but rather in order to get some better ideas about what *necessarily* grows out of what. How a thing works is only fully revealed when its changes are understood and its ancestry comprehended. What implies what? What determines what? What are the necessary conditions for the development of something else?

So which is more important, ancestry or function? The answer to this must be that a study of ancestry from a functional point of view leads to fuller understanding of the function, and of course a study of function from the point of view of ancestry helps in understanding of the ancestry. These things together are the evolutionary point of view. What about history? Isn't that ancestry? Yes, often people seem to mean specific evolution or phylogeny by the word "history." But more usually history is merely the data: we dug this up and it was in township and range such-and-such; Columbus actually came in 1492, not 1493. Functionalism and evolutionism are not data; they are theoretical contexts into which data are placed. But history is not theoretical except when specific evolution is miscalled by that name.

Nevertheless, the history that disturbed Radcliffe-Brown was clearly not *data* in the above perfectly usual sense in which history has been used. Rather, it seems apparent that ideas and theories ("conjectures") of origin, growth, adaptation, and alteration of culture through time were what he rejected, inconsistent though this may seem with his statement quoted earlier that seems to recommend evolutionary studies. But that statement approves of the study of *social* evolution, not cultural evolution. The stultification of theory caused by the taboo of the concept culture is very real and very serious, for it is not merely history (in any of its meanings) that is ignored but history-of-culture, or culture-history, as related to evolution.

One of the main arguments that this book offers is that culture has uses, as a concept, in discussing causes, dependencies, and necessities in evolutionary change. Also, it has been argued here that structure is a result of various processes, even when this conception includes kinship statuses as well as groups. This is one of the main reasons why pure functionalism will never get at anything basic, even after the libraries are flooded with structural-functional analyses. Structure cannot cause *itself*. A more generously-conceived entity—culture—seems required, as does a temporal dimension.

Further, the attempt was made to show more specific relational priorities. The basic evolutionary changes in primitive social organization seem to begin with adaptive selection of cultural rules of social behavior—mainly rules of marriage, marital residence, and of classifications of people —which then affect the structure of residential groups. Then new rules, again, go into making sodalities under varying specific adaptive circumstances. And these, too, can react back on the residential groups. It was even argued that the concept of true descent as applied to groups came about in sodalities first. Changes in the status network are consequent upon prior changes in any or all of the foregoing, but this relationship is often indirect and is complicated by the fact that still other considerations such as rank, specialization, political position, and a host of others, also can have something to do with status positions.

But there is still no way to prove that the causal chain argued in this book is True and that others must be False. The choice must involve a judgment on the related premises, notions, and concepts implicit in cultural evolutionary theory which were tried out in the attempts at conjectural history. Either they work out in such a way that intellectual satisfaction is increased or they do not. It is up to the reader to decide on that basis, because few available data can be used in ways that fully test the theory or any of its particular assumptions or hypotheses.

With respect to comparison of cultural evolutionism and

functionalism, then, the present book is an extended argument rather than a proof. The purpose has been to show that cultural evolutionary theory can illuminate data, scanty or not, in ways that nontemporal, noncultural, functional theory cannot. In fact, it could be argued that logically functional theory (alone) cannot even pose the question of cause. *If* more light is cast, or more widely cast, by evolutionary theory, then it does not matter at this moment if the facts are wrong for they can be corrected, nor really whether the theory and the classification are as yet all that has been claimed for them, nor if they are misapplied or used unintelligently. As more facts come in, as the theory is improved by others, and as it is used with more logic and intelligence, we should gain a better understanding of function itself, and particularly of causal dependence and necessity among the parts of culture. And among those parts and aspects of culture may be included social organization in general and social structure in particular.

Bibliography

ABERLE, DAVID F. (1967). "A Scale of Alternate Generation Terminology," *Southwestern Journal of Anthropology* 23:26.

ADAM, LEONHARD (1947). "Virilocal and Uxorilocal," *American Anthropologist* 49:678.

ADAMS, RICHARD N. (1960). "An Inquiry into the Nature of the Family," in Gertrude E. Dole and Robert L. Carneiro (eds.), *Essays in the Science of Culture in Honor of Leslie A. White*. New York: Crowell.

ADAMS, ROBERT MC C. (1966). *The Evolution of Urban Society*. Chicago: Aldine.

AGINSKY, BURT W., and PETER H. BUCK (1940). "Interacting Forces in the Maori Family," *American Anthropologist* 42:195.

ANDERSON, ROBERT (1960). "Reduction of Variants as a Measure of Cultural Integration," in Gertrude E. Dole and Robert L. Carneiro (eds.), *Essays in the Science of Culture in Honor of Leslie A. White*. New York: Crowell.

ARENDT, HANNAH (1961). *Between Past and Future*. New York: Viking.

ARENSBERG, CONRAD M. (1957). "Anthropology as History," in Karl Polanyi, C. M. Arensberg, and H. Pearson (eds.), *Trade and Market in the Early Empires*. New York: Free Press.

ASCHMANN, HOMER (1959). "The Central Desert of Baja California: Demography and Ecology," *Ibero-Americana* 42. Berkeley and Los Angeles: University of California Press.

BARNES, J. A. (1960). "Marriage and Residential Continuity," *American Anthropologist* 62:850.

BEATTIE, J. H. M. (1957–1958). "Nyoro Kinship, Marriage, and Affinity," *Africa* 27:317, 28:1.

BEFU, HARUMI and LEONARD PLOTNICOV (1962). "Types of Corporate Unilineal Descent Groups," *American Anthropologist* 64:313.

BIDNEY, DAVID (1953). *Theoretical Anthropology*. New York: Columbia University Press.

BINFORD, SALLY R., and LOUIS R. BINFORD (1968). *New Perspectives in Archaeology*. Chicago: Aldine.

BIRDSELL, JOSEPH B. (1970). "Local Group Composition Among the Australian Aborigines: A Critique of the Evidence from Fieldwork Conducted since 1930," *Current Anthropology* 2:115.

BOAS, FRANZ (1888). *The Central Eskimo*. 6th Annual Report of the Bureau of American Ethnology. Washington, D.C.: U.S. Government Printing Office.

BOHANNAN, PAUL (1958). "Political Aspects of Tiv Social Organization," in John Middleton and David Tait (eds.), *Tribes Without Rulers*. London: Routledge.

BOLTON, HERBERT E., ed. and tr. (1950). *Pageant in the Wilderness*. Salt Lake City: Utah Historical Society.

BUCKLES, WILLIAM G. (1960). *An Ethnohistorical Approach to Anthropological Research*. Unpublished ms.

CARNEIRO, ROBERT (1967). "On the Relationship Between Size of Population and Complexity of Social Organization," *Southwestern Journal of Anthropology* 23:234.

——— (1969). "Ascertaining, Testing, and Interpreting Sequences of Cultural Development," *Southwestern Journal of Anthropology* 24:354.

CASSIRER, ERNST (1944). *An Essay on Man*. New Haven: Yale University Press.

CHILDE, V. GORDON (1946). *What Happened in History*. Baltimore: Penguin Books.

CLARK, J. DESMOND (1960). "Human Ecology during Pleistocene and Later Times in Africa South of the Sahara," *Current Anthropology* 1:307.

CODERE, HELEN (1957). "Kwakiutl Society: Rank without Class," *American Anthropologist* 59:473.

COOPER, JOHN A. (1946). "The Yahgan," in J. H. Steward (ed.), *Handbook of South American Indians I: The Marginal Tribes*. Bureau of American Ethnology Bulletin 143. Washington, D.C.: U.S. Government Printing Office.

COUES, ELLIOT, ed. (1897). *New Light on the Early History of the Greater Northwest: The Manuscript Journals of Alexander Henry and David Thompson, 1799–1814*. 3 vols. New York: Harper & Row.

——— (1900). *On the Trail of a Spanish Pioneer*. 2 vols. New York: Harper & Row.

COUNT, EARL W. (1958). "The Biological Basis of Human Sociality," *American Anthropologist* 60:1049.

CURTIS, EDWARD S. (1928). *The North American Indian* 18. Norwood, Mass. Plimpton.

DOBBS, ARTHUR (1744). *An Account of the Countries Adjoining to Hudson's Bay*. London: J. Robinson.

DOLE, GERTRUDE E. (1957). *The Development of Patterns of Kinship*

Nomenclature. Ph.D. Dissertation. Ann Arbor: University Microfilms.

DRUCKER, PHILIP (1939). "Rank, Wealth, and Kinship in Northwest Coast Society," *American Anthropologist* 41:55.

DUNNING, R. W. (1959). *Social and Economic Change among the Northern Ojibwa.* Toronto: University of Toronto Press.

DURKHEIM, EMILE (1933). *The Division of Labor in Society.* New York: Free Press.

—— (1938). *The Rules of the Sociological Method.* New York: Free Press.

EDMONSON, MUNROE S. (1958). *Status Terminology and the Social Structure of North American Indians.* Seattle: University of Washington Press.

EGGAN, FRED. (1937). "Historical Changes in the Choctow Kinship System," *American Anthropologist* 39:34.

—— (1950). *Social Organization of the Western Pueblos.* Chicago: University of Chicago Press.

—— (1955). "Social Anthropology: Methods and Results," in Frederick Eggan (ed.), *Social Anthropology of North American Indian Tribes,* 2nd ed. Chicago: University of Chicago Press.

EISENSTADT, S. N. (1954). "Plains Indian Age Groups: Some Comparative Notes," *Man* 54:6.

ELKIN, A. P. (1931). "The Dieri Kinship System," *Journal of the Royal Anthropological Institute* 61:493.

—— (1932). "Social Organization in the Kimberly Division, Northwestern Australia," *Oceania* 2:296.

—— (1954). *The Australian Aborigines: How to Understand Them.* Sydney and London: Angus and Robertson.

EPLING, P. J. (1967). "Lay Perception of Kinship: A Samoan Case Study," *Oceania* 37:260.

EVANS-PRITCHARD, E. E. (1940). *The Nuer.* Oxford: Oxford University Press.

—— (1951). *Kinship and Marriage among the Nuer.* Oxford: Oxford University Press.

FATHAUER, GEORGE H. (1942). *Social Organization and Kinship of the Northern Athabaskan Indians.* M.A. Dissertation, University of Chicago.

FIRTH, RAYMOND (1930). "Marriage and the Classificatory System of Relationship," *Journal of the Royal Anthropological Institute* 60:235.

—— (1936). *We, the Tikopia.* New York: Macmillan.

—— (1951). "Contemporary British Social Anthropology," *American Anthropologist* 53:474.

—— (1957). "A Note on Descent Groups in Polynesia," *Man* 57:4.

FORDE, C. DARYLL (1947). "The Anthropological Approach in Social Science," *The Advancement of Science* 4:213.

FORTES, MEYER (1953). "The Structure of Unilineal Descent Groups," *American Anthropologist* 55:17.

FRIED, MORTON H. (1957). "The Classification of Corporate Unilineal

Descent Groups," *Journal of the Royal Anthropological Institute* 87:1.

———— (1960). "On the Evolution of Social Stratification and the State," in Stanley Diamond (ed.), *Culture in History: Essays in Honor of Paul Radin*. New York: Columbia University Press.

———— (1966). "On the Concepts of 'Tribe' and Tribal Society," *Transactions of the New York Academy of Sciences*, Series II, 28:527.

———— (1967). *The Evolution of Political Society*. New York: Random House.

GOLDMAN, IRVING (1955). "Status Rivalry and Cultural Evolution in Polynesia," *American Anthropologist* 57:680.

GOLDSCHMIDT, WALTER (1948). "Social Organization in Native California and the Origin of Clans," *American Anthropologist* 50:444.

———— (1959). *Man's Way*. New York: Holt, Rinehart and Winston.

———— (1960). *Exploring the Ways of Mankind*. New York: Holt, Rinehart and Winston.

GOODENOUGH, WARD H. (1955). "A Problem in Malayo-Polynesian Social Organization," *American Anthropologist* 57:71.

GOODY, JACK (1961). "The Classification of Double Descent Systems," *Current Anthropology* 2:3.

GREENBERG, JOSEPH H. (1959). "Language and Evolution," In *Evolution and Anthropology: A Centennial Appraisal*. Washington, D.C.: Anthropological Society of Washington.

GUSINDE, MARTIN (1955). "Pygmies and Pygmoids: Twides of Tropical Africa," *Primitive Man* 28:3.

HART, C. W. M., and ARNOLD R. PILLING (1960). *The Tiwi of North Australia*. New York: Holt, Rinehart and Winston.

HENRY, ALEXANDER (1809). *Travels and Adventures*. New York: Riley.

HERSKOVITS, MELVILLE J. (1955). *Cultural Anthropology*. New York: Knopf.

HICKERSON, HAROLD (1960). "The Feast of the Dead among the Seventeenth Century Algonkians of the Upper Great Lakes," *American Anthropologist* 62:81.

HOCART, A. M. (1928). "The Indo-European Kinship System," *Ceylon Journal of Science*. Section G. *Archaeology, Ethnology* 1:179.

———— (1931). "Alternating Generations in Fiji," *Man* 31:222.

———— (1955). "Kinship Systems," in Hoebel, Jennings, and Smith (eds.), *Readings in Anthropology*. New York: McGraw-Hill.

HUGHES, CHARLES C. (1958). "An Eskimo Deviant from the 'Eskimo' Type of Social Organization," *American Anthropologist* 60:1140.

IMANISHI, KINJI (1960). "Social Organization of Subhuman Primates in Their Natural Habitat," *Current Anthropology* 1:393.

JAY, PHYLLIS C., ed. (1968). *Primates: Studies in Adaptation and Variability*. New York: Holt, Rinehart and Winston.

KINIETZ, VERNON W. (1940). *Indians of the Western Great Lakes*. Ann Arbor: University of Michigan Press.

KIRCHHOFF, PAUL (1955). "The Principles of Clanship in Human Society," *Davidson Anthropological Journal* 1:1. Reprinted in Fried,

Morton H., ed. (1959). *Readings in Anthropology,* 2 vols. New York: Crowell.

KRADER, LAWRENCE (1955). "Principles and Structures in the Organization of the Asiatic Steppe-Pastoralists," *Southwestern Journal of Anthropology* 11:67.

KROEBER, ALFRED L. (1909). "Classificatory Systems of Relationship," *Journal of the Royal Anthropological Institute* 39:77.

LANE, BARBARA S. (1960). "Varieties of Cross-Cousin Marriage and Incest Taboos: Structure and Causality," in Gertrude E. Dole and Robert L. Carneiro (eds.), *Essays in the Science of Culture in Honor of Leslie A. White.* New York: Crowell.

LANE, ROBERT B. (1961). "A Reconsideration of Malayo-Polynesian Social Organization," *American Anthropologist* 63:711.

LANG, ANDREW (1907–1908). "The Origin of Terms of Human Relationship," *Proceedings of the British Academy.* London.

LEACH, E. R. (1951). "The Structural Implications of Matrilateral Cross-cousin Marriage," *Journal of the Royal Anthropological Institute* 81:23.

LEACOCK, ELEANOR (1955). "Matrilocality in a Simple Hunting Economy (Montagnais-Naskapi)," *Southwestern Journal of Anthropology* 11:31.

LEE, RICHARD B. (1968). "What Hunters Do for a Living, or How to Make Out on Scarce Resources," in Lee and DeVore: 30.

——and IRVEN DE VORE (eds.) (1968). *Man the Hunter.* Chicago: Aldine.

LESSER, ALEXANDER (1961). "Social Fields and the Evolution of Society," *Southwestern Journal of Anthropology* 17:40.

LÉVI-STRAUSS, CLAUDE (1949). *Les structures élémentaires de la parenté.* Paris: Presses Universitaires de France.

—— (1966). "The Future of Kinship Studies," *Proceedings of the Royal Anthropological Institute of Great Britain and Ireland for 1965* 13.

LOUNSBURY, FLOYD (1965). "A Formal Account of the Crow- and Omaha-Type Kinship Terminologies," and "Another View of Trobriand Kin Categories," in E. A. Hammel (ed.) (1965). *Formal Semantic Analysis,* Special Publication, *American Anthropologist* 67, No. 5, Part 2:142.

LOWIE, ROBERT H. (1928). "A Note on Relationship Terminologies," *American Anthropologist* 30:263.

—— (1948). *Social Organization.* New York: Rinehart.

MAC KENZIE, ALEXANDER (1802). *Voyages.* Philadelphia: John Morgan.

MC LENNAN, JOHN F. (1886). *Studies in Ancient History.* London and New York: Macmillan.

MAC NEISH, JUNE H. (1960). "Kin Terms of Arctic Drainage Déné: Hare, Slavey, Chipewyan," *American Anthropologist* 62:279.

MAC NEISH, RICHARD (1964). "Ancient Mesoamerican Civilization," *Science* 143:No. 3606.

MAINE, HENRY S. (1861). *Ancient Law.* London: J. Murray.

MALINOWSKI, BRONISLAW (1913). *The Family among the Australian Aborigines.* London: University of London Press.

—— (1930). "Parenthood, the Basis for Social Structure," in Victor F. Calverton and Samuel D. Schmalhausen, eds., *The New Generation.* London: Macaulay.

MAN, E. H. (1932). *On the Aboriginal Inhabitants of the Andaman Islands.* London: The Royal Anthropological Institute of Great Britain and Ireland.

MARTIN, M. KAY (1969). "South American Foragers: A Case Study in Cultural Devolution," *American Anthropologist* 71:243.

MASSEY, WILLIAM C. (1961). "The Cultural Distinction of Aboriginal Baja California," in *Homenaje á Pablo Martínez del Rio.* Mexico, D.F.: Instituto Nacional de Antropología e Historia.

MEGGITT, M. J. (1968). " 'Marriage Classes' and Demography in Central Australia," in Lee and DeVore 176.

MORGAN, LEWIS H. (1871). *Systems of Consanguinity and Affinity of the Human Family.* Smithsonian Institution Contributions to Knowledge. Washington, D.C.: U.S. Government Printing Office.

MURDOCK, GEORGE P. (1947). "Bifurcate Merging, A Test of Five Theories," *American Anthropologist* 49:56.

—— (1949). *Social Structure.* New York: Macmillan.

—— (1951). "British Social Anthropology," *American Anthropologist* 53:465.

——, ed. (1960). *Social Structure in Southeast Asia.* Viking Fund Publications in Anthropology 29.

MURPHY, ROBERT F. (1956). "Matrilocality and Patrilineality in Mundurucu Society," *American Anthropologist* 58:414.

NEEDHAM, RODNEY (1956). Review of Homans and Schneider, 1955, *American Journal of Sociology* 62:107.

OBERG, KALERVO (1955). "Types of Social Structure among the Lowland Tribes of South and Central America," *American Anthropologist* 57:472.

PARSONS, TALCOTT (1943). "The Kinship System of the Contemporary United States," *American Anthropologist* 45:22.

PEHRSON, ROBERT N. (1954). "Bilateral Kin Grouping as a Structural Type: A Preliminary Statement," *University of Manila Journal of East Asiatic Studies* 3:199.

PFEIFFER, JOHN E. (1969). *The Emergence of Man.* New York: Harper & Row.

POWELL, JOHN W., and G. W. INGALLS (1874). *Report on the Condition of the Ute Indians of Utah; the Pai-Utes of Utah, Northern Arizona, Southern Nevada, and Southeastern California; the Go-Si Utes of Utah and Nevada; the Northwestern Shoshones of Idaho and Utah; and the Western Shoshones of Nevada.* Washington, D.C.: Report of the Commissioner on Indian Affairs for 1873:41.

RADCLIFFE-BROWN, A. R. (1948). *The Andaman Islanders.* New York: Free Press.

—— (1952). *Structure and Function in Primitive Society.* New York: Free Press.

——— (1956). "On Australian Local Organization," *American Anthropologist* 58:363.

RIVERS, W. H. R. (1907). "On the Origin of the Classificatory System of Relationships," in *Anthropological Essays Presented to Edward Burnett Tylor*. Oxford: Oxford University Press.

——— (1914). *Kinship and Social Organization*. London: Constable.

ROSE, F. G. G. (1968). "Australian Marriage, Land-Owning Groups, and Initiations," in Lee and DeVore 200.

ROSS, ALEXANDER (1956). *The Fur Hunters of the Far West*, edited by Kenneth A. Spaulding. Norman, Oklahoma: University of Oklahoma Press.

SAHLINS, MARSHALL D. (1958). *Social Stratification in Polynesia*. Seattle: University of Washington Press.

——— (1959). "The Social Life of Monkeys, Apes, and Primitive Men," in Morton H. Fried (ed.), *Readings in Anthropology* 2 vols. New York: Crowell.

——— (1960). "The Origin of Society," *Scientific American*, September: 76.

——— (1961). "The Segmentary Lineage: An Organization of Predatory Expansion," *American Anthropologist* 63:322.

——— (1962). *Moala: Culture and Nature on a Fijian Island*. Ann Arbor: University of Michigan Press.

——— (1968). *Tribesmen*. Englewood Cliffs, N.J.: Prentice-Hall.

———, and ELMAN R. SERVICE, eds. (1960). *Evolution and Culture*. Ann Arbor: University of Michigan Press.

SANDERS, WILLIAM T., and BARBARA J. PRICE (1968). *Mesoamerica: The Evolution of a Civilization*. New York: Random House.

SCHEFFLER, H. W. (1966). "Ancestor Worship in Anthropology: Or, Observations on Descent and Descent Groups," *Current Anthropology* 7:541.

SCHNEIDER, DAVID M. (1967). "Descent and Filiation as Cultural Constructs," *Southwestern Journal of Anthropology* 23:65.

SERVICE, ELMAN R. (1960). "Kinship Terminology and Evolution," *American Anthropologist* 62:747.

——— (1960a). "Sociocentric Relationship Terms and the Australian Class System," in Gertrude E. Dole and Robert L. Carneiro (eds.), *Essays in the Science of Culture in Honor of Leslie A. White*. New York: Crowell.

——— (1970). *Cultural Evolutionism: Theory in Practice*. New York: Holt, Rinehart and Winston.

SLATER, MIRIAM K. (1959). "Ecological Factors in the Origin of Incest," *American Anthropologist* 61:1042.

SPICER, EDWARD H., ed. (1961). *Perspectives in American Indian Culture Change*. Chicago: University of Chicago Press.

SPOEHR, ALEXANDER (1947). "Changing Kinship Systems: A Study in the Acculturation of the Creeks, Cherokee, and Choctaw," *Field Museum of Natural History Anthropological Series* 33:151.

STEFANSSON, VILHJALMUR (1914). *The Stefansson-Anderson Arctic Expedition of The American Museum: Preliminary Ethnological Report,* Anthropological Papers of the American Museum of Natural History 14, pt. 1.

———— (1919). *My Life with the Eskimos.* New York: Macmillan.

———— (1927). "Eskimos," *Encyclopaedia Britannica,* 14th ed.

STEWARD, JULIAN H. (1938). *Basin-Plateau Aboriginal Sociopolitical Groups.* Smithsonian Institution Bureau of American Ethnology Bulletin 120. Washington, D.C.: U.S. Government Printing Office.

———— (1948). "The Circum-Caribbean Tribes: An Introduction," in J. H. Steward (ed.), *Handbook of South American Indians 4, The Circum-Caribbean Tribes.* Smithsonian Institution Bureau of American Ethnology Bulletin 143. Washington, D.C.: U.S. Government Printing Office.

———— (1955). *Theory of Culture Change.* Urbana: University of Illinois.

————, and LOUIS C. FARON (1959). *Native Peoples of South America.* New York: McGraw-Hill.

SUTTLES, WAYNE (1960). "Affinal Ties, Subsistence, and Prestige among the Coast Salish," *American Anthropologist* 62:296.

SWANTON, JOHN R. (1946). "The Indians of the Southeastern United States," *Smithsonian Institution Bureau of American Ethnology* Bulletin 137, Washington, D.C.: U.S. Government Printing Office.

THALBITZER, WILLIAM, ed. (1914). "The Ammassalik Eskimo," *Meddelelser om Grønland* 39.

THOMAS, ELIZABETH MARSHALL (1959). *The Harmless People.* New York: Knopf.

THOMAS, N. W. (1906). *Kinship Organization and Group Marriage in Australia.* Cambridge, England: Cambridge University Press.

TITIEV, MISCHA (1943). "The Influence of Common Residence on the Unilateral Classification of Kindred," *American Anthropologist* 45: 511.

TURNBULL, COLIN M. (1961). *The Forest People.* New York: Simon and Schuster.

TYLOR, EDWARD B. (1888). "On a Method of Investigating the Development of Institutions; Applied to Laws of Marriage and Descent," *Journal of the Anthropological Institute* 18:245.

———— (1894). "On the Tasmanians as Representatives of Paleolithic Men," *Journal of the Anthropological Institute* 23:141.

TYRELL, JOSEPH B., ed. (1916). *David Thompson's Narrative of His Explorations in North America.* Toronto: The Champlain Society.

————, ed. (1934). *Journals of Samuel Hearne and Philip Turnor.* Toronto: The Champlain Society.

WAGLEY, CHARLES (1940). "The Effects of Depopulation upon Social Organization as Illustrated by the Tapirape Indians," *Transactions of the New York Academy of Science* (ns.) 3:12.

WALLACE, ANTHONY F. C. (1961). "On Being Just Complicated Enough," *Proceedings of the National Academy of Sciences* 47:458.

―――― and JOHN ATKINS (1960). "The Meaning of Kinship Terms," *American Anthropologist* 62:58.

WARNER, W. LLOYD ([1937] 1964). *A Black Civilization.* New York: Harper & Row.

WASHBURN, SHERWOOD L. (1957). "Australopithecines: the Hunters or the Hunted?" *American Anthropologist* 59:612.

―――― (1960). "Tools and Human Evolution," *Scientific American,* September:63.

―――― (1960a). *Populations of Baboons.* Paper delivered at American Anthropological Association, 59th Annual Meeting, November 17–20. Minneapolis.

――――, PHYLLIS JAY, and J. B. LANCASTER (1965). "Field Studies of Old World Monkeys and Apes," *Science* 150 (3703):1541.

WILBERT, JOHANNES, ed. (1961). *The Evolution of Horticultural Systems in Native South America: Causes and Consequences.* Caracas: Sociedad de Ciencias Naturales La Salle.

WINICK, CHARLES (1956). *Dictionary of Anthropology.* New York: Philosophical Library.

WITTFOGEL, KARL A. (1957). *Oriental Despotism.* New Haven: Yale University Press.

WHITE, LESLIE A. (1949). "The Symbol: The Origin and Basis of Human Behavior," in L. A. White, *The Science of Culture,* Ch. II. New York: Farrar, Straus. Paperback ed., New York: Grove Press, London: Evergreen Books.

―――― (1959). *The Evolution of Culture.* New York: McGraw-Hill.

YENGOYAN, A. A. (1968). "Demographic and Ecological Influences on Aboriginal Australian Marriage Sections," in Lee and DeVore 185.

ZUCKERMAN, SOLLIE (1932). *The Social Life of Monkeys and Apes.* London: Kegan Paul, Trench, Trubner.

Index